THE CHRISTIAN RELIGION
& ITS COMPETITORS TO-DAY

T0382187

THE CHRISTIAN RELIGION & ITS COMPETITORS TO-DAY

BEING THE HULSEAN LECTURES FOR 1924–5 DELIVERED BEFORE THE UNIVERSITY OF CAMBRIDGE

by the Rev.

A. C. BOUQUET, D.D., Hon. C.F.

FORMERLY A SCHOLAR OF TRINITY COLLEGE
AND A LADY KAY SCHOLAR OF JESUS COLLEGE
VICAR OF ALL SAINTS CAMBRIDGE

CAMBRIDGE
AT THE UNIVERSITY PRESS
1925

CAMBRIDGE UNIVERSITY PRESS
Cambridge, New York, Melbourne, Madrid, Cape Town,
Singapore, São Paulo, Delhi, Mexico City

Cambridge University Press
The Edinburgh Building, Cambridge CB2 8RU, UK

Published in the United States of America by Cambridge University Press, New York

www.cambridge.org
Information on this title: www.cambridge.org/9781107623576

First published 1925
First paperback edition 2013

A catalogue record for this publication is available from the British Library

ISBN 978-1-107-62357-6 Paperback

TO

MY FATHER
IN HIS
EIGHTY-THIRD YEAR

CONTENTS

PREFATORY NOTE

THE LECTURES are printed almost exactly as they were spoken, except for the addition of a few passages which had to be cut out in delivery in order to save time. A sermon preached in substance to undergraduates at Queens' College is appended. The news of the death of Baron Friedrich von Hügel comes just as I am revising the book for press. As he is quoted several times in the course of the lectures, the very least I can do is to add my humble tribute of respect to a great Christian whom I remember with gratitude as a kind and courteous neighbour and counsellor during the three years after the war when I was working in London. I should like to acknowledge also the great help I have received from my wife and from some of the younger members of my congregation in preparing the MS. for publication.

A. C. B.

O Thou Who art the everlasting Essence of things beyond space and time and yet within them; Thou Who transcendest yet pervadest all things, manifest Thyself unto us, feeling after Thee, seeking Thee in the shades of ignorance. Stretch forth Thy hand to help us who cannot without Thee come to Thee; and reveal Thyself unto us who seek nothing beside Thee; through Jesus Christ our Lord. Amen.

JOHN SCOTUS ERIGENA

THE CHRISTIAN RELIGION AND ITS COMPETITORS TO-DAY

LECTURE I

INTRODUCTION

The subject of these lectures is "The Christian Religion and its competitors to-day."

Rivalry may seem to imply antagonism, and I can therefore imagine one of the numerous believers in universal tolerance exclaiming, not without irritation: "Here is again a case of the odious Christian engaged in attacking other religions than his own." I can assure such an objector that I do not believe in universal tolerance any more than he does, although as an upholder of freedom of thought and opinion I do not wish to send him to the stake for calling me an odious Christian. His attitude of easy indifference to truth I cannot praise, and I propose to attack it with all the earnestness of argument at my disposal. For the moment, however, he may rest, and we will make our beginning by setting down the following facts, which the more thoughtful individual will readily accept.

Homo Sapiens, as he looks back over the development of his career upon this planet, observes that among other features he has evolved the sense of what has been called a "felt practical relationship with what is believed in as a super-human being or beings." (1) This sense has guided him to some of his greatest achievements, and on the whole he values it. He finds it difficult to believe with thinkers like Jung (2) and Simmel (3) that it is a reaction towards an imaginary being, "a mere psychological function of an irrational nature," since in normal cases it shows no association with insanity, and is rich in positive fruits (4); and he declines to draw generalisations from abnormal cases of psychopathology. Nevertheless this sense is a delicate one, in its intenser forms very unequally distributed, easily repressed and even extinguished, and only capable of growth and endurance after much care and training. It is indeed like a precious flower growing up amid the traffic of some public highway, always in peril of being trodden down and crushed out of existence.

In the world of to-day, fraught with a multitude of changes, thoughtful persons will wish to take stock and to discover where religion stands in the face of secularism, and if it still stands, from what system of faith and practice they may reasonably hope for guidance in facing the future. Can the Christian system still offer them all that they need or will ever need?

I make some small apology for seeming to be an enthusiast for religion in an atmosphere which is noted for its sobriety and reserve. Religious interest is as much a part of my personal as Shakespeare is of our common heritage. My father's family, if you can forgive the reference, left their native land for conscience sake, and the churchwarden's staff has seldom departed from between the feet of my maternal forbears, who seem as London citizens to have produced not only a pious tailor, one John Stow of Cornhill, who gave up his business to write history in the days of Queen Elizabeth, but also an undistinguished Dean of St Paul's when Henry IV was King. The interest is therefore hereditary, and I cannot cut it out of my life. To anyone here present who shares not the same experience and thinks me prejudiced, I tender such expressions of regret as may seem due.

The fortunes of peace and war have caused your lecturer to temper his academic studies with a rather larger degree than is usual of pastoral and practical experience. He is proud and glad to have done so, since the materials for any real view of the significance of religion lie as much in the lives of men and women as in books. Books, it is true, recall and crystallise the experiences, testimonies and reflections of living persons, and serve to diffuse and transmit the reasonings and speculations of original thinkers, but no one who has explored the alcoves of the Cockerell building can doubt that most books about religion are but ephemeral things, and that eight out of every ten, even of the best, contribute but meagrely to our understanding of the wonder and splendour and mystery of the spiritual life. The great mass of mankind are indeed the living epistles of God. In their struggles and experiences may be read His purpose and His character. There are in one sense no ordinary people. Each individual is fresh and distinct. A system of doctrine framed wholly in terms of the divinity school or theological college must inevitably prove as inadequate as abstract theories of science woven independently of the laboratories of Downing Street. Just as in the medical profession the real training for a specialist lies in the handling and observation of as many cases as possible, so I believe the best part of the training of a specialist in religion consists in the personal handling and observation of as great a variety as possible of cases of religious experience. I doubt the value of questionnaires as compared with the knowledge gained from a pastoral career, and I am not ashamed to confess that my interest in Christianity is in a living and creative religion actually at work building the character of individuals, still expanding, still developing, still making history—for such it certainly is.

The limitations of space and time plainly preclude a lengthy treatment of any subject, and seem almost to invite a detailed essay covering only a little ground. But there are serious objections to the adoption of this course. The appeal of a detailed essay is likely to be limited, and signs are not absent that a lecturer on this foundation is expected to keep in view a wider circle than would be affected by a highly technical treatise, and a larger and less learned audience than frequents university sermons.

It seems best, therefore, to try to give a connected account of the modern case for religion, and of the reasons why among our younger generation there are those who wage an offensive for the spiritual supremacy of Jesus of Nazareth with renewed passion and enthusiasm. I ask your prayers that what is said may be uttered in a spirit of charity and reasonable humility.

Spiritual values, as we have already had reason to remark, are compelled to struggle for their existence.

Four main alternatives are offered to our world to-day, and it will be our task to consider each of them in turn.

1. In the first place, there is secularism, or no religion at all.

2. In the second place, there is pantheism, or God everywhere, so that the individual soul becomes an illusion, or at any rate ceases to be ultimate, while the course of history does not count.

3. In the third place, there is traditionalism, or a steady reversion to popular paganism under a Christian veneer.

4. In the fourth place, there is relativism, or the rejection of any positive creed as final, on the ground that religious truth is still polymorphous, so that the absolute religion lies hid deep in the womb of the infinite future.

Let us analyse each of these in turn and see what it has to offer, and try to estimate its value.

SECULARISM

The word secularism was, I believe, coined in 1851 by George Jacob Holyoake, to describe his own neutral and agnostic system of thought and practice in order to distinguish it from the rampant atheism of Bradlaugh. To-day, however, we apply it more loosely to describe a group of widely differing organised movements or vague tendencies, all of which emphasise the finite and concrete world or saeculum, and ignore the possible existence of the spiritual or infinite. The best motto to describe all these is that of the French encyclopaedist: "La question de Dieu manque d'actualité," but of course their main idea is at least as old as the Psalm in which we read of "The foolish body who said 'there is no God.'"

There are various paths by which this attitude is reached, and they deserve some notice.

It is the fashion to-day to speak of the religious consciousness as either the working of a single faculty, or the alignment of the total number of human faculties upon the most important element in man's environment, and to say that man is a religious animal, or more correctly is capable of becoming a religious animal. Attention is concentrated by psychologists upon the expression of the religious emotions, the reason, and the will, as testifying to the felt presence of the Divine. Man is able to establish contact and relationship with point after point in his environment, and in that environment the highest point is said to be God.

"Man," it has been said,(5) "is placed in a real environment, not an imaginary one. If there was no Being in man's environment to which the conception of God in some measure corresponded, man would not best succeed in adjusting himself to his environment by belief in God. Such a belief as this would be entirely quixotic in its effects....But the opposite is the fact. Therefore there is a God": and again the late Mr Bernard Bosanquet says(6): "The instinctive appetite or demand for God...is a proof of the reality of Deity, in the same sort of sense in which hunger is a proof of the existence of food, or the sexual impulse proof of the existence of possible mates. Of course obvious exceptions take place: you may starve; you may die unmated. But *in rerum natura* an instinct implies an object; and if you find a special emotional impulse, such as that of worship and religion, which pervades all sorts of particular experiences, but maintains its unique suggestions and demand throughout them all, you can hardly help recognising the object of this emotion as at least some peculiar feature of the world."

When we give our attention to these matters we cannot fail to observe that there are a number of curious lapses in the working of the religious consciousness.

It is probably true, as Mr Bernard Shaw says (in the preface to *Androcles*), that mankind may be divided into three classes: the keenly religious at one extreme, the anti-religious at the other, and the indifferent between the two. In the central mass, to which the majority of persons belong, the God-consciousness is very dim, and almost entirely unused except at rare intervals.

The commonest cause of secularism is the existence of competing interests in life. Man, as Baron Friedrich von Hügel quaintly reminds us, begins by being a "land animal," (7) whatever he may afterwards become. Perhaps we like better Dean Beeching's poetic conception of the boy as

> Nimble and light of limb
> In three elements free
> To run, to ride, to swim.

(If the poet had lived longer he would doubtless have mended his verse to work in a fourth.) Anyhow the main interests are eating, sleeping, falling in love, fighting, marrying, getting the better of your neighbour, hunting, ranging about the earth, and working off spare energy in some form of play.

From time to time however a new element appears, whether it be a mild form of mystical experience, or a glimmering of the moral consciousness. It is easy for such a new element to be swamped by its fellows, and it can only maintain its footing by one of two devices. It may either drive the other interests completely into the background, and entirely dominate life, or it may inter-penetrate the other interests, moulding and transforming them as it does so. The former device may be said to adopt the vertical and the latter the horizontal arrangement of life. The vertical arrangement acquiesces in the existence of many interests, and is prepared to confine the practice of religion to persons of a particular temperament. The horizontal arrangement involves the recognition that the whole of human life deserves a religious alignment, and would link a religious motive to almost every human interest or activity. It will be clear at once that the vertical or departmental arrangement ends logically in the career of the monk or nun, so that those who adopt the secular career simply practise their religion by proxy or ignore it altogether. The horizontal arrangement, while admittedly more attractive, runs the risk of bringing religion into every department of life, but at the price of lowering its standard.

The history of religion both in public and private provides a series of illustrations of the fluctuation between these two courses of action. One of the puzzles that the psychologist does not yet seem to have finished studying is that which is presented by the phenomenon of a great and, as it would seem, compelling interest first of all becoming central in the life of a human being, and then more or less gradually moving away and ceasing to be central.

The problem is not altogether one of religion. It may be compared with the fact that large sections of human society live in a state of more or less permanent dissociation from things of which there is no reason to doubt the value, truth, or beauty. Absence of an aesthetic sense is very widespread. Many savages as well as many civilised persons have no appreciation of a fine landscape, and do not care for flowers. The respect due to natural scenery is not to be taken for granted. The instinct to make kitchen-middens is deep rooted in humanity, and it remains yet to be seen whether a really democratic government can protect any country-side from disfigurement and pollution. (Attempts up to the present, whether made at Versailles or in Richmond Park, seem to have been a failure.) A taste for music, painting and good literature is, oddly enough, much less freely distributed than the impulse to worship. Truth and accuracy, cleanliness and a devotion to hygiene are unhappily still absent from the lives of the majority of the two-legged humans who cluster upon this rolling sphere. Political indifference is really quite as great as religious indifference. Lord Bryce in his survey of Modern Democracies (8) seems to view their future in a twilight of misgiving because he cannot feel confident that their citizens will remain interested enough in the institutions they have acquired to work them honestly and well. Thus, for example, in the General Election of 1918 a large South-London division, with a register of 37,322, only sent 29 per cent. of its electors to the poll, while in 600 constituencies only 58 per cent. of the total votes were polled. And this was a Victory Election, which was intended to present the ministers who had carried the country through her trials with a vote of confidence and of gratitude. To pursue this line of argument: In the General Election of last year there was a heavy average poll, somewhere about 72 per cent., but this is, I believe, a high record, and is on a par with Church attendance at a Harvest Thanksgiving or a Friendly Societies' parade, and in any case some 6,000,000 persons did not trouble to vote. In the French elections of 1906, out of about eleven and a half millions of electors, over six millions did not trouble to record their votes. The recent heavy polling in England is again exceptional, and in municipal elections the interest rarely rises beyond the point of bringing 25 per cent. of electors to the poll. A conference in South-London was recently organised to discuss problems of juvenile unemployment with parents. Leaders of all three political parties were present, and 5000 invitations were issued to ordinary citizens, but only thirty attended!

It is beyond dispute that human beings seldom

remain throughout life in a steady contact with all points in their environment. Attention may shift curiously with changing circumstances. There have been periods of history during which the general average of attention to some important topic has fallen conspicuously low. Thus it is probable that when artistic taste was at its lowest in England during the earlier middle part of the nineteenth century, institutional religion was relatively strong. Taste has now improved, while the practice of devotional exercises in public has declined, though it is still enormously stronger than it was in the year 1800, when there were only six communicants in St Paul's Cathedral on Easter Day, and the Oxford movement had not begun. Pastoral experience shows that among habitual believers there are very strongly marked fluctuations in the religious consciousness, the origin of which cannot in all cases be accurately determined, though in an appreciable number it admits of fairly easy diagnosis. We all have our phases, and in one we may read a particular class of novel or attend concerts frequently, in another may never buy or borrow a single piece of fiction or hear a note of orchestral music. Such a change does not postulate the unreality of the lending library or make the achievements of Glazounoff and Ravel an hallucination. It only involves a shifting of the centre of attention and interest. This shifting or transference of interest is to some degree connected with sex and age. Thus at the age of thirteen a human male will often be found, as we know, keenly interested in some form of acquisitiveness whether directed towards stamps or butterflies. At twenty-one he will be the proverbial peacock. At forty-five he may run the risk of becoming an embittered cynic. His religious interest varies accordingly, and the pendulum tends to swing between storm and calm, between healthy-mindedness and sickness of soul. The fluctuations of religious interest among women and girls may also be associated with the physical conditions peculiar to maternity and spinsterhood.

It is commonly said that the most favourable period for conversions is that which lies between the ages of eighteen and twenty-five, and some would even make it begin earlier. In later life the pressure of worldly tasks, the increasing burden of competition, and the fierceness of the struggle for existence deprived until recently all except the really leisured classes of any genuine opportunity to cultivate either religious worship, music, art, literature, or even politics. In his parable of the sower, Jesus of Nazareth, who "knew what was in man" points out that not more than one out of every four individuals may be expected to bring spiritual fruit to perfection. Even in the case of persons of leisure, the swing of the pendulum of attention is noticeable as much in religious affairs as in any other. It is indeed curious how ill-health, marriage, success in business, the birth of a child, or change of neighbourhood, will in turn drive in or divert all outward expression of religious interest. I once visited a sick hospital nurse who had completely abandoned religion because a doctor had jilted her. The case was an almost exact parallel to that of the Sunday School teacher mentioned in Dr Hart's *Psychology of Insanity* (9). What may be called *frequency* in the expression of religious sentiment is also no doubt largely determined by the climate of a district or of the season of the year, and by the like or dislike of change. Human beings are either creatures of habit or lovers of variety, and hence they tend to express or inhibit their religious emotions in accordance with a spirit of radicalism or conservatism.

It is safe therefore to conclude that a large amount of secularism is no organised movement but is due to the pressure of competing elements in life. The seed sown among thorns is a complete picture of this sort of secularist danger. The cares and riches and pleasures of life may threaten to choke spiritual religion, but they are a casual growth, and have not necessarily been planted round the seed by some sinister and malicious conspiracy. The inventor of the first motor engine need not have been a militant atheist. But the enlargement of man's physical organs due to applied science (which has almost literally given him new eyes, ears, arms and legs) has resulted in making his spiritual institutions seem too small. Moreover this same applied science has provided the human family with such a galaxy of new toys that, like busy children in a nursery intent on their play, they have no time left in which to take notice of the kindly parent to whose inspiration the inventions were originally due. The glamour of mechanical contrivances has for the time blinded them to the existence of the *mysterium tremendum*.

I think the point has now been reached at which it is necessary to enter a protest against the tendency to attribute a strong religious interest to man in his early stages of development. A great deal of what is dealt with as religion in comparative textbooks really seems to be primitive science, that is to say, attempts to account for the order and operations of a visible but pluralistic universe, rather than at establishing unselfish and disinterested relations with the one good God. Animism in its lower or higher forms is only a description of the forces of nature. The spirits, daemons, or deities, to employ Prof. Leuba's phrase, are *used*. Human interest is for the most part secular. There is little or no devotion to the Deity as an end in Himself, as the embodiment of the highest moral and spiritual values. Sacrifices are offered by the ancient farmer for the same object that the modern one employs chemical manures, and for no other. It is precisely for this reason that in the famous dialogue, Euthyphro finds it so difficult to answer Socrates, when he asks "What is the good of the cultus?" because Socrates has already cut away the connexion between the Gods and natural phenomena. The Parisian Catholic undergraduate makes a votive offering to the Immaculate Virgin for success in his examination, where the Cambridge Protestant merely employs a good coach. But is there any real difference in the dominant interest? It seems to me that vital religion to-day, instead of having

shrunk, is still as ever running its course in a very
narrow groove, just as Harnack has always declared
it does. All that science has done is to force the
indifferent or self-centred to be honest. Vital religion
only begins when the worshipper can cease merely
to pray, "O God give," and say "O God teach,"
or "O God guide," or "O God use me." In fact,
what the best instincts of the world to-day are
willing to recognise as worthy religion hardly appears until we get in sight of an ethical and spiritual
monotheism. Till that point it is utilitarian and
anthropocentric, and whether daemons, or Burmese
nats, or at the other end of the scale the mythical
St Christopher, "protecteur des voyageurs," be the
centre of devotion, the object of the cultus remains
merely to carry on the machinery of society and
conserve material values.

The importance of this point can hardly be over-
estimated. Certain men of science have in the past
been disposed to regard the religious faculty as just
an animistic interpretation of nature, certain to be
displaced by education, so that religion must indeed
inevitably transform itself into philosophy. But I
venture to suggest that if we know anything to-day
about the age of the human race (while it may be
that "religion" in the strict sense is merely the
relationship of the parts to the whole and to one
another, and is not confined to human beings, and
is quite certainly primitive), whatever is worth
calling spiritual theistic religion is a relatively late
development, and belongs less to man's infancy than
to his prime. A widespread reversion to secularism

on the part of the cruder species of humanity as among the industrial proletariat only means that a reaction towards animism is impossible for those who have had a modern secular education, but does not mean that the official abandonment of moral theism is an advance. Similarly the abandonment of moral theism for a pessimistic philosophy, were it to spread from certain individuals to whole classes of society, would denote senility of the race rather than ripeness. Even Guyau's irreligion of the future is a kind of positivist mysticism: it is not really atheism. Philosophic secularism is the creed of persons stranded on a barren lee-shore. It is only fair to insist that a proportion of apparent secularism on the part of serious persons is in reality the exact opposite. It is a logical form of Quakerism, in which all life becomes religious, and in which therefore the reservation of one part for church-going or formal cultus seems unnecessary. In many respects (though not in all) this policy deserves praise, since it seeks to consecrate every human activity and to penetrate it with the spirit of religion, but it makes great demands on the individual, demands which at present the bulk of mankind do not seem ready to concede.

There is of course another type of secularism which is more highly organised, and it is with that that we must next proceed to deal. It may be said to derive itself from four main sources. The first of these is the comparatively aristocratic rationalism which developed in patches about Europe during the seventeenth century and increased in volume

during the eighteenth. The second source is the
volcanic outburst of indignation against a corrupt
established society with which the eighteenth century
ended. That society, after persecuting a perfectly
sincere attempt to purify Catholic Christianity, had
ended by producing a state of affairs in which the
entire population conformed to catholicism while
scarcely anyone believed in it, and from such an
elaborate hypocrisy the reaction was bound to be
furious. The third and more recent source is the
levelling influence of industrialism. No more potent
force has ever existed for the obliteration of spiritual
values than the factory system. The monotonous accumulation of ugly buildings, ponderous machinery,
rows and blocks of workmen's dwellings and enormous
piles of waste products has gone on and still goes
on all over the planet. With modifications and local
improvements the same type of activity charac-
terises the steel works of Shanghai and Pittsburg
and the mills of Osaka and Bombay. There is now
very little difference to the casual traveller between
Amiens and Swindon. The fourth source is the
spread of state-aided secular culture, including a
fair smattering of natural science, and an entire
absence of appeal to independent authority as
against investigation.

The leisured and professional classes may flatter
themselves that they have emerged from mid-
Victorian materialism into a re-acceptance of spiritual
values. But they are living in a fool's paradise. You
cannot have State education for three generations
without a good deal of ferment. When a communist

said the other day to an English bishop, "I don't think much of God's management of the world," he was simply reflecting the new attitude toward traditional authority which prevails from school-children upwards. You cannot grow human beings in an atmosphere of urban industry for the same period without unrest. It was always predicted that when the man in the street succeeded in absorbing the theory of the origin of species there would be trouble. He has now done so, and it is having precisely the result that was prophesied.

In 1859 Darwin published the first edition of his famous work. In 1847 Marx and Engels wrote their Manifesto of the Communist Party (10). This brief and extremely able statement of a point of view which Marx afterwards expounded at length in *Das Kapital* still seems to be the basis of all communist propaganda. Engels wrote some years later a special preface to the authorised English translation, in which he quite frankly connected Darwinism and Marxism, and declared the latter to be the natural consequence of the former.* A recent pamphlet emanating from Glasgow represents a member of the Independent Labour Party and a member of the Communist Party (although debating against one another) as both accepting the following state-ment (11):—"In all general evolutionary progress the keynote is struggle; struggle of various and several kinds, struggle between species and species, between species and genus, between both species

* Chronologically, if in no other way, this is of course inaccurate.

and genus and category, struggle between all of them. There is an intensive struggle going on all the time; and the human race is not and never has been any exception to that general evolutionary rule." According to these pamphleteers economic struggle is the key to history. The capitalist organisation of society, having superseded the old feudalism and patriarchal aristocracy, presents the world with the spectacle of two main classes, the bourgeois and the proletariat, the propertied and the property-less. Marx and Engels and their followers regard the eighteenth century rationalism as the downfall of religion, and believe the whole of the bourgeois organisation of institutional religion since that period to be a gigantic piece of fraud designed to give a sort of divine sanction to the bourgeois supremacy, and to hinder the proletarians from opposing it, by appealing to their superstition. There is only one logical interpretation of history, say they, and that is as the conflict of classes in human society, corresponding to the conflict of species in animal society. Nature *is* "red in tooth and claw with ravin" and it is not only the little wood, but the city as well which is "a world of plunder and prey." There are two main classes or species of human beings, and the proper and inevitable course is for the one to fight and overcome the other, just as has happened in the case of the black and brown rat.

This doctrine is not pleasant reading, especially if one happens to be a bourgeois, and we shall have occasion to point out presently that it is both obsolete and inadequate, but it is brutally frank, clear, and easy to understand. It obviously makes an immense appeal to the vast masses of wage-earners who inhabit the grimy and depressing cities of industry, and the stuffy cottages of some of our villages, because it claims to offer them relief from what they quite rightly call the wretched and over-crowded conditions in which many of them are condemned to live, and it comes to them with the supposed sanction of the blessed phrase "modern science."

I wonder whether any of my hearers have wit-nessed as I have one of the great May Day demon-strations in London. They are of course relatively small in England to what they are on the continent, but even in Hyde Park they can be impressive. To see men, women and children marching in wide ranks for a whole hour, with the constant repetition on banner and car of the Marxian formula: "Workers of the world unite, you have nothing to lose but your chains," is to receive the impression of a by no means negligible force. Let us remember that the bulk of continental socialists are not moderates such as till recently predominated in this country, but are much more Marxian and anti-clerical. Con-tinental labour is chiefly confronted with an ob-scurantist Christianity. It is not surprising therefore that the communist programme as circulated in-cludes the following paragraphs: "Under the head of combating bourgeois prejudices and superstitions the first place is to be taken by the fight against religion, a fight which must be carried on with all

requisite tact and all caution especially among those
sections of workers in whose daily life religion has
hitherto been deeply rooted" (12). . . . "The new culture of a humanity united for the first time and
having now abolished all limits set by intermediate
state forms will be founded on clear and reciprocal
relations among human beings. It will thus bury *all
mysticism, religion and superstition*"* (notice the
combination) "for all time, and give a mighty forward impetus to the development of all-conquering
human mind." (13)

In Germany more than in any other country
except Russia the masses of the workers are de-
claring themselves convinced of the correctness of
the communist attitude. So serious has this become
that in reaction the middle-classes in Prussia have
vigorously urged the abandonment of the complete
separation between Church and State, whether
wisely or not remains to be seen. In France as also
in Czecho-Slovakia the communist party contains
the majority of the politically organised workers,
and France under her present government is now
seeking to secularise the scout movement, a movement which, certainly in its origin, was definitely
theistic. The situation in Russia needs no comment.
Russia has cast in her lot with Asia rather than
Europe, and "the New Islam" is extending its propaganda into China as well as other newly won
areas of the Christian mission-field (14). In America
and Canada labour is regarded as rather backward
in organisation, but Russian extremists penetrate

* The italics are my own.

thither, and we know that after the war for a short time a soviet actually existed in Winnipeg. In this country there is a steady land-slide in the direction of extremer views. In Glasgow at a post-war by-election 11,000 persons voted for a candidate who accepted the full Moscow programme. I once asked a leading representative of labour the reason for this defection from the pieties of northern Presbyterianism. He replied, "Go and look at their housing conditions."

I do not regard the political events that have taken place since this lecture was written as greatly modifying the general religious situation. The labour anti-clericals remain such, even if they have been outvoted, and their time will come again later.

It is of course not impossible to combine communism with religion, but the attempt is seldom made. I think it is reasonable to point out however that More in his *Utopia* (not exactly a recent work) frankly accepts a kind of communism as part of the teaching of Jesus Christ, imparted to the Utopians by Hythloday and his companions. "Howbeit I thinke this was no smale helpe and furtherance in the matter, that they harde us say, that Christ instituted among his, al things commen; and that the same communitie doth yet remaine amongest the rightest Christian companies." (15) After an extensive search I have only succeeded in discovering one pamphlet, representing a communist group centred round Lille, which, after describing what a communist organisation of society will be like, offers the reader a sketch of the life of Christ based rather

oddly on the writings of Loisy, and not unreasonably claims the sanction of the New Testament
(especially the early chapters of Acts) for its
theories (16). There are said to be as many as
eighteen Christian communist sects in the United
States, but they do not appear to exercise any
important influence.

The study of natural science as a source of actual
secularism is doubtless on the wane, for those who
know enough about it. It must be plain that
theories of relativity (among other developments)
have destroyed the absolute claim made by mechan-
istic conceptions of the universe. A religious interpretation of nature has as good a right to be true
as any other. Even many scientists who repudiate
orthodox or conventionalised religion of whatever
sort will still own to the possession of some kind of
private faith. They will probably not be Christians,
and they may have difficulties about adulatory
worship, and think our church services, with the
principles of which they have only a superficial
acquaintance, to be mere "puja." But nevertheless
they cannot and they do not wish to ignore the
spiritual hunger which compels them to seek for
truth and goodness and beauty at whatever cost,
and to live as devotees of the highest that they
know.

It is still true, however, perhaps increasingly true
in a university, that "a little natural philosophy,
and the first entrance to it doth dispose the opinion
to atheism," (17) and that a half-hearted and dilet-
tante prosecution of scientific study may simply

disintegrate the flimsy structure of conventional Christianity which many a young student brings away from his public school, while his consequent lapse into a careless secularism is likely to have a sinister effect upon his fellow citizens, the younger of whom especially are ready to take their tone from him. And even this is not all that may be said. Though the rest of the quotation "and on the other side much natural philosophy, and wading deep into it will bring man's mind to religion," [18] may be cited to encourage us, the uncomfortable fact must be faced that when (for example) Mr Julian Huxley invents a religion for himself [19] it is not centred upon Christ at all, while even the weighty scientific conference held at Oxford this year, under the auspices of the modern Churchmen, got nowhere near the old orthodox Christianity of, let us say, Bishop Westcott's day; and we know when we are honest with ourselves, that however earnestly and long its members may pursue their quest they never will, for the old order is passing away for ever.

There are several types of secularists who deserve more sympathy from religious people than they usually get. Among such are all who suffer from fatigue, nervous reaction or mental depression due to illness, or whose atheism is the direct result of a repressed complex or an inversion. Other such are earnest iconoclasts. Ordinary religion with its shibboleths has to them grown cheap. Words, they say, are but symbols and there is an idolatry even in dogma. Better to believe in what God stands for than to call Him by a name which has become both

tarnished and trivial. Others revolt against an
obscurantist religion which disgusts them, and
seeking vainly for an alternative, exclaim finally:
"There is nothing in religion at all but shams and
old wives' fables." There are also those who find
it difficult to believe in an actively benevolent
Deity, and are flung back upon atheism and so
upon secularism by the evil and suffering in the
world. To them I would say at once, "Do not think
that we ask you primarily to believe in the Deity
of Christ. We invite you rather to believe in
the Christianity of God, and in the ultimate
victory of such a God as the only alternative to
that radical pessimism which destroys the entire
value and meaning of the world of phenomena and
makes our individual spirits mere luckless units in
the midst of a misfortune from which there is no
escape save in extinction (if that be possible)."

There are finally those who have suffered evil at
the hands of religious people, or who feel that the
dice are always loaded against them. From Prome-
theus to Dick Dudgeon, one's heart warms to such
people. Karl Marx himself is probably an instance (20). Born a German Jew, and no doubt the
victim of anti-Semitic venom, by a curious fatality
he found himself in childhood baptised willy-nilly
as a Lutheran Protestant. His friendship with the
younger Hegelians did not prevent him from
being expelled from his university for ultra-radical
opinions. Further expulsions from continental cities
led to his exile in this country, where he lived in
some squalor in Soho and had the mortification to

see most of his children die young. His collected
instances of sweating and capitalist oppression (all
of them unfortunately English) differ very little
from any which might be found in the research
files of the Christian Social Union, and it is curious
to reflect how near he came to us when we read
that some of the most scandalously insanitary
cottage dwellings which he condemned were at
Gamlingay, in this very county of Cambridge (21).

I regret that there is no time to speak in detail
of the very serious secularisation of the modern
sovereign state, in which the Church is simply one
of a number of voluntary corporations, but a former
Hulsean Lecturer has ably dealt with this in one
of his later essays (22). I must, however, say a word
regarding the curious departmentalisation of life
which is the reflection of this policy in daily affairs.
Has it ever struck any of my hearers that the view
of a vast mass of persons who minister to our needs
to-day is utterly departmental? We go into a
London restaurant, and see a bevy of sprightly and
smartly dressed waitresses. They are obviously
selected for their good looks and vivacity of manner.
But can we picture them (no longer wearing their
distinctive livery) kneeling beside us in our own
parish churches? Does their tone suggest that there
is any connexion between Christianity and res-
taurants? The answer must be that with a few
exceptions most of them convey to us the impression of a cheerful secularism, encouraged perhaps
by having persistently to stand about and watch
other human beings eat. Leaving this restaurant

we enter an electric tube. Is it easy to picture the ticket-puncher or door-slammer as punching or slamming to the glory of God? I fear we must confess that there are whole tracts of industry, commerce, and domestic service which stand almost completely outside the sphere of religion. The extremest cases one can conjure up are those of a builder's labourers engaged in erecting a theological college, when their actual interest in it is simply as a building, and of the men who tune organs and erect stained-glass windows, who generally seem to take an entirely detached view of the purpose for which organs are played or painted windows erected.

Having now briefly analysed the various types of secularism, it is time to consider in what ways those persons who value religion may meet and deal with them.

First in order I would put the need of much greater frankness. I do not see what useful purpose can be served by people who disagree with the religious interpretation of the world pretending that such disagreement does not matter. If one believes any sort of religion to be true, and spiritual values to be more than mere psychological phenomena, then such religion and such values must be the greatest facts in life. They can take no second place. If, however, one holds all religion to be false, then to treat it with polite indifference is most ignoble, since such indifference may be confused with silent assent or tolerance. Moreover, the ramifications of religious influence in life are so many and varied that if it is a harmful thing, then its baneful effects are bound

to be so widespread that it ought to be everywhere
uprooted. I welcome the frankness of the communist. A frank enemy is at all times preferable to
a false friend. It is possible to convert the former,
but not the latter, since at the root of his soul sticks
that most damnable of all lies—that indifference
does not matter. I appeal to all persons who are
at present indifferent to face up to the situation
and to treat the issue "secularism or religion"
seriously, and if they disagree to do so with passion,
and not in an anaemic way. I desire therefore to
begin being frank here and now, and if I thereby
draw the enemy's fire, I care but little.

What single virtue can secularism claim as the
result of disregarding spiritual values? Or is it perhaps that secularism proposes a new scale of values?
If so, what are they? Let us see them in order that
we may compare them with the old. Does the
secularist character really display at its average
greater beauty than that character which is the
fruit of religious training, of whatever kind? Is a
life from which all spiritual values have been
deliberately excluded and in which all responsibility
to a higher power has been extinguished really a
higher life than the one in which a sense of reverence
and obligation is dominant? Are the children of a
secularist school more attractive human beings than
those of a school where an intelligent faith prevails?
Are the people who with self-conscious superiority
neglect those simple actions of devotion and prayer
which socially express their relationship to a Divine
Being really an advance upon their ancestors?

We yet await convincing answers to such questions. I look in vain during my pastoral work for any sign that the new unorganised secularism or this-worldliness produces a new beauty of character or preserves the values of the religious system which it has casually dropped. Its votaries do not really differ from the worldly people of past ages. For one honest agnostic saint who abandons the practice of his religion through intensity of scruple, there are, I fear, a hundred persons who abandon it through sheer laziness, through the love of money or success, through a deadly self-complacency or lack of humility, or through the delusion that self-pleasing is the secret of the universe. Some, alas! are rationalisers, and are just making the pretence of atheism a camouflage for secret sin or a sorrow they would fain forget. I see no evidence that the policy of repressing the religious faculty is producing a better race of human beings, while it appears that even secularist teachers who endeavour to inculcate atheistic ethics in elementary schools have, in many cases, recourse to an appeal to "conscience" in their pupils. This of course is only a muffled form of religion, a pagan Quakerism that dares not call itself by its real name. The effects of secular education in Australia and the United States do not seem to have been specially encouraging. Troeltsch's remarks about "Atheistische Ethik" are, I think, quite just, and suggest that something really has got left out of the scheme of life in which it prevails, since "For the recognition of the definitely ethical content of life," as he points out, "there is no scientific solution." (23)

And next to frankness I would place sympathy and sincerity. For those who really care, and are puzzled, I would have us all take infinite pains, and try to help them in every way we can. More folk than many of us reckon are sad to-day because they would like to have something to satisfy their ineradicable longing for a decent religion, and if they are gay it is with a forced gaiety—and that is also camouflage! I have here no compendium of new theology to offer such people. It is still in the making. But I believe God can be trusted to make Himself plain, and that we clergy will serve our friends best by being honest and sympathetic, and showing that what we care most about is to get at the truth at all costs, and that we want them to share with us this quest for God, in which also we are sure that we have some things which we can impart to them without presumption, and of which we feel no reason to be ashamed.

In the third place, let us insist upon a serious enquiry into the importance of spiritual values. The remedy for unorganised secularism is the ministry of conversion.

The indifference with which many people regard the teaching and claims of religion may be due to an uneasy consciousness that if they come too close they may be compelled to surrender some private selfishness which they cherish. But only too many fail to come close enough even to estimate its importance, or to realise the possibility of its capturing them in the end. Bishop Butler's warning is needed again in our generation. The negligence in religious matters of many otherwise intelligent persons can only be described as contemptible. It is astounding to note how beggarly are the mental habits of many men. From stock-broking to golf, from golf to stock-broking, from the machine to the football ground, from the stadium back to the mill; where in such lives can a place be found for the stupendous riches of the spiritual life? What wonderful treasures and adventures these people are missing. How obvious it is that something essential is being left out of their daily round of existence. I must confess that I do not think the religious consciousness is capable of becoming permanently central any more than the consciousness of any other element in life. The preservation of its centrality is the real aim in the pastoral work of the church, and is an art by itself, an art worth learning and practising.

In the fourth place, the time is ripe for an entirely fresh re-casting of our methods of religious teaching in school and college. St Augustine's "ex amante alio accenditur alius" (24) is now a commonplace, and it is abundantly clear to-day that we cannot foster a deep loyalty to spiritual values by perfunctory bible-reading or formal chapel attendance. No one can catch from us what we have not already made our own, and when every other lesson in school is based on reasoning and proof, the religious instruction, if it is merely authoritarian, must certainly fail to get home. The only pastors and teachers who can have any right to give a scripture lesson or to conduct worship must be those in whom the spiritual life is a working reality and who can pass it on to others. More harm than can easily be estimated has accrued in the past from forcing men and women to undertake duties in which they themselves were not really interested. Unconverted school teachers (using the adjective in its deepest sense) can actually damage the young souls in their charge. Their influence is not neutral. Far more important than any bible syllabus or catechism over which we may easily disagree is the actual witness of the teacher by honest prayer and consistent example to the reality of religion as interpreting the whole of life in and out of school. Perhaps I speak to some who mean to be or are already schoolmasters. Let such beware of the peril of regarding religion as a "subject" like chemistry. Religion is not a "subject." It cannot be pigeon-holed. Instead, it should be a spirit and temper animating and pervading every human occupation. One is often tempted to wonder what would happen if the House of Commons could be persuaded to sit in Quaker silence before entering upon the discussion of a controversial measure, or the competitors in the Olympic games partake of a united Communion before the opening of the contests. Much might be done to expel secularism by interweaving the highest and most intelligent and moral acts of devotion among the details of common life. It is said that the pre-revolution Russians did so. But they appear to have associated the practice with so much magic and superstition as to discredit the entire structure of religion in the eyes of thoughtful persons.

And what of the secularism produced by scientific

study? Here there are two plain remedies. On the one hand there must be a greater wholeness of view, and less departmentalisation in education, for vocational training (so-called) is ever in danger of making the student neglect the significance of the whole wood in favour of a detailed knowledge of a few of its trees. On the other hand, whatever talk there may reasonably be about "discontinuities," "transilience," or "levels of organic life," the notion of a God who works in gaps and intervenes at uncertain intervals must be banished from the popular expression of Christianity, as it has largely disappeared from its best theology. If we claim the whole field of life for God the Holy Spirit in theory, let us also do it in liturgy and practice.

The conflict with highly organised political secularism is by far the most serious which has ever faced the Christian Church or indeed any other religious body. It is difficult to believe that it can be successfully waged by repressive measures such as blasphemy laws and seditious teaching acts, or by alliance with any political party. That is not the policy by which a good and honest religion has in the past won its way. Let us fight, but fight openly, and by fair means. If, as we believe, our doctrine is of God, we can trust it to prevail over error. We have recently been reminded that just as the world resisted Christ, so it is not impossible for it to resist a Christ-like Church. Only let us take care that the Church really is Christ-like (25). Let us without the use of technicalities and well-worn phrases emphasise that if God exists there is every good reason for identifying His character with the character of Jesus Christ. He is the window by which we can look into the mind of the Being who rules the universe, and Calvary and all that it stands for is the largest light in the window. Let us make it clear that that is the real bedrock principle of Christianity, and let us alter our official confessions and simplify our liturgies so as to render the expression of that principle less obscure and complicated than it is at present. Let us teach and practise (in the open as much as ever we can) with all possible clearness the New Testament view of personality and property, the dignity, sanctity and worth of the individual soul, the universal duty of service in useful work, and the stewardship of goods. There is no excuse for allowing secularist pamphlets to appropriate such good Pauline texts as "If any man will not work neither let him eat," as though they had been invented in Moscow (26).

There are two further elements in the teaching of the New Testament which are obviously superior to those of the Marxian communist, and which need courageous emphasis. The first of these is the recognition of the solidarity of society known as the brotherhood of man. The Marxist cannot honestly hold this dogma any more than the extreme diehard imperialist, since he believes in domestic as fervently as his opponent believes in international struggles. It is true that in his programme he advocates "the abolition of classes, and of class-war, the energy thus released to be employed in the struggle with nature, and for the progress and de-

velopment of the power and dominion of mankind."
But this really means the extermination by slow or
rapid means of all who do not belong to a particular
group of human beings. The Christian believes in
conversion rather than in extermination, and he has
a strong objection to the hypocritical limitation of
brotherhood to the white races (27). The second
element in New Testament teaching which needs
emphasis is the recognition that although society
is one body, all men have not the same office.
Differentiation of functions does not, it is true, entitle
any persons in any class to remain idle and un-
productive, but it does contradict the curious error
of the Marxian secularist in supposing that the
highest values in the world can be conserved by
the preservation of one species, the *ouvrier*. It must
be plain that the highest values in the world can
only be conserved by properly protecting the brain-
worker, and by encouraging the development of a rich
variety of human types, the utility of all of which may
not be immediately obvious to cruder intelligences.

The obsolete nature of the popular secularist
teaching about the struggle for existence needs such
careful exposure as I can hardly hope to undertake
here and now. Four or five points may however
briefly be emphasised.

Darwin took the idea of the struggle for existence
from the individualist industrialism of his day, and
applied it to animal life. To apply it therefore by
transference from animal to human life is to argue
in a circle, and even so, war among human beings is
not primitive.

Struggle in animal life though important is not its dominant element. Accommodation and co-operation are equally important. The struggle where it exists is much more struggle against the circumstances of climate and weather than against other creatures. Even then there is often a truce with nature, and the attainment of a static condition.

The oft quoted instance of the black and brown rat is no instance at all, because *the brown rat has not exterminated the black*. There has merely been a compromise, and they have divided the ground between them.

Self-sacrifice and co-operation are quite as important items in animal life as struggle. The disharmonies and shadows as admitted by Prof. J. A. Thomson are not nearly so important as some would make them. Even if they were, we should be back again at Huxley's famous assertion that the cosmic process was so unpleasant that the best man could do would be to change its order and substitute other and more genial principles. But they are not. Nature has more to say than "Everyone for himself." There has been a selection of the other-regarding, of the self-sacrificing, of the gentle, of the loving....We see the success of self-sacrifice, the rewards of love, the stability of societies.

The popular philosophy of class struggle is therefore to be rejected as a distortion of fact. Those who seek a detailed refutation must look for it in the pages of modern biological research (28). One can only add that the case of those of us who stand for any sort of religion is that we are men and not merely land animals, and that we believe in a spiritual nisus, an "upward and onward" towards a future which is not materialistic. We "dare to think that spiritual life in man is the revelation of creative reality." (29) And we will apologise for this to no croakers.

I hope in this matter that I have spoken fairly. No one has a right to judge the secularist agitator harshly who has not himself felt the pressure of having to labour for an undiscerning and unimaginative employer, who has not been out of employment through no fault of his own or who has not been inadequately fed, housed or paid in return for honest work well done. I utterly repudiate the idea that the clergy are bound necessarily to side with the bourgeois. They are as little bound to side with the proletariat. It is their business in life as far as is humanly possible to avoid identifying themselves with the interests of any single class, and to discourage class-consciousness wherever they encounter it. But it is also their duty to try hard to see the truth as it really is and to speak it without fear or favour, and especially to insist that a man's life under all circumstances consists not in the abundance of the things which he possesses. I have no patience with the sickly hypocrisy of the rich and worldly politicians and their followers who denounce the bolshevik persecution of Christianity, but who show no real interest in the vital Christian movement of this country. I believe that if they were not afraid of injuring the fabric of their own vested interests by destroying organised Christian effort they would be just as openly hostile to it themselves.

I desire to advocate in conclusion the federation

as far as practicable of all persons of whatever creed who believe in maintaining a proper emphasis upon spiritual values. We shall not be able to walk all the way together, but let us at least walk as far as we can. This proposal was made as far back as the fifteenth century by St Nicholas of Cusa, and is therefore quite a respectable one. There is indeed more common ground between an earnest Hindu, an earnest Moslem, an earnest Jew, an earnest unclassified mystic, and an earnest Christian of any denomination, than between any one of these five and a secularist whose chief aim is material prosperity. We need much greater earnestness upon the part of classified adherents of religion. So long as this country has professedly religious men to rule it, and does not repudiate the public recognition of religion in state affairs, its citizens have a right to expect that the Government will exercise a strict protection of the hours of worship, preserve young persons and children from pernicious influences, and safeguard, for those who labour, their right to one complete day of leisure every week, since the essence of Sunday is leisure, even if it be misused—leisure as the phrase goes, "vacare Deo."

Let me end by urging that the keenest weapon against secularism is for the advocates of religion to preach and practise the noblest possible conception of God. Professional hypocrisy, cheap certainty, and unsympathetic shepherding are still responsible for a very great deal of honest secularism, which is the natural reaction against an official, muffled, and lifeless expression of Christianity. There is only one real danger which men of faith need fear, and that is that the doctrine of God offered by his ministers to the world should not be true enough or good enough to be worth believing. God has granted us such knowledge of Himself as may satisfy the noblest aspirations. If the human race is to starve for experience of the Divine, it must needs starve in the midst of plenty. Let those of us who minister in spiritual things see that we do not proclaim to our hearers less than the very best it has been given man to know, for a mean creed is the greatest enemy of religion.

PANTHEISM

THOSE of you who may have thought your lecturer somewhat militant last week will find themselves to-day in a more tranquil atmosphere. We are to consider the claims of a rival system of religion, or rather, having sorted our society into two classes, religious and secularist, we are to examine the former, and debate as I hope in a friendly spirit the relative merits of the two main types which it contains, since it is better, we argue, to hold any form of religion than none at all. In case someone feels that the topic is not of practical interest, let me first venture to explain why it has been chosen. It is perhaps superfluous to define a term so generally understood as pantheism, but I prefer to avoid any possible misunderstanding and therefore give the following, in which a recent writer on the subject outlines in familiar terms its fundamental tenets: "Nothing is which is not God, and God is everything that is. There can be no other source of being than God, and no other power than His. We and the rest of the universe are but phases of His Being. Nothing can be conceived as having even temporary separation from Him. God and the universe must be identified, and if any part of the universe cannot be identified with Him, that part must be negated." [1] It is unnecessary to refer to the immense populations of Asia which swing between pantheism and polytheism, but those whose every day life brings them chiefly face-to-face either with the various well-recognised Christian denominations or with mere secular indifference will hardly be conscious of the wide and ever-increasing fascination which pantheism in some form or other exercises in the modern western world. This influence, though increasing, is not new. Goethe indeed declared perhaps rashly that "all antiquity thought in this way." It is at any rate quite certain that a large part of the world to-day thinks in pantheistic terms, and it would be foolish and short-sighted as well as discourteous to many earnest and religious fellow-citizens not to recognise the fact. Writers such as Mr Allanson Picton (who, I believe, represent a fairly large constituency) try to construct a sort of Christian pantheism, which they call "The religion of the universe," (2) and which finds its symbolic representation in a picture which a few years back had a considerable vogue called: "The Omnipresent." But further, the inclination of scientific thinkers when they have pressed beyond mere descriptive analysis to speculate upon origins has also tended to the formation of a pantheistic philosophy, such as that of Herbert Spencer. The spiritual monism of more recent times is another notable instance of this tendency, though, after all, monism is a term which may be used to embrace all pantheistic thinkers from Plotinus, who was a mystical monist, to mediaeval mystics such as the lady Julian whose aim is "to noughten all else that is made for to love and have God that is unmade." (3) In the words of a Scotch professor, "The aim of the

rapturous devotion of the saint is just to be able
to possess one's soul...as a phase of God. If the
mystic can say with sincerity 'God is all' he feels
he has reached his goal. He feels that he is enabled
to reach the highest level of religion, and in becoming
conscious of the identity between himself and God,
his soul is satisfied with the possibility of absolute
devotion." (4) Even those who instead of saying "God
is all" prefer to say "All is God" find their emotions
captivated by the thrill of devotion which the im-
mensity of the conception calls forth. Spinoza is the
striking instance of a Jewish pantheist, a materialistic monist with a touch of mysticism. Hegel is the
intellectualistic monist who explains everything in
forms of thought. Schopenhauer and von Hartmann
embrace a monism of cosmic will which sub-
merges the individual. And so we come down to
the *Monisten-Bund* of Haeckel and the monistic
catechism, from which I shall presently quote a few
extracts. I admit that there are objections to the
identification of materialistic monism with pantheism, for the *one* of Haeckel's monism has not
such a degree of theistic colouring as would warrant
comparison of it with the *one* of the pantheist. But
since Haeckel wrote his *Riddle of the Universe* many
changes have swept over the world of science, and
the monism of to-day is quite definitely much more
spiritual. "We have only to be completely logical,"
says one biologist, "and believe that something of
the same general nature as mind exists in all life,
to make the further step and believe that it exists
even in the matter from which life sprang. In that

case we would have to enlarge our definition of
matter, for the properties of 'matter' that is to say
the world-stuff would include mind." It is of course
this "enlargement of the definition of matter" (5)
which is significant, though care must be taken not
to confuse pantheism with the doctrine of Divine
immanence.

It must be plain then that the attractiveness of
pantheism to-day lies in two features. In the first
place, it claims to satisfy the religious sense of mankind while at the same time avoiding a theology
of gaps. In the second place, it denies the necessity
of a single historical revelation, and so seems to cut
the knot of the problems associated with creeds and
Scripture and the appeal to antiquity, since it is
possible to be a devout pantheist and to be entirely
ignorant of the past, and there are many who feel
the difficulty of connecting religion with historical
events.

Some would even go so far as to say that pantheism
is the logical outcome of Lutheran Protestantism,
which makes religion base itself primarily upon an
experience within the soul. It is certain that the
reaction against Scripture springing from the apparent uncertainty given to its meaning by the
growth of biblical criticism has flung men back upon
themselves. The popular reaction from dogmatic in
favour of experimental religion which began by re-
taining the Jesus of History is now in some quarters
inclined to revert to purely mystical experience, and
to regard the Deity as a fixed and changeless entity
whom each individual is to discover afresh for

himself, or a changing Being whose experience runs along with and is involved in our own experience. To each individual the revelation must come separately. "What to me is another man's knowledge?" said a young soldier a few years ago: "I want to know for myself." The conventional impatience at dogma is of two kinds. There is first the objection to dogma which seems false. Dogmas of science, where well attested, are accepted with almost superstitious reverence. There is in the second place impatience of dogma as inherited tradition and as opposed to the immediacy of experimental research.

Those of us who are ministers of religion cannot fail to be aware that among our congregations as well as among the people we visit are many persons for whom knowledge of past history and interest in it are unimportant things. Our people recognise that some specialists should study history because experience of past events may guide rulers and politicians in the avoidance of possible future mistakes, but such experience can only affect religion on the assumption that the Divine hand is equally evident in all historical happenings, since there are no gaps, and God is not more in one human life than in another.

I think I can illustrate this popular stand-point best by repeating an imaginary conversation which appeared some ten years or so ago in the pages of *Punch*, and which has been quoted more than once.

UNCLE: "Hate all your lessons? Come now you don't mean to say you hate history?"

CHILD: "Yes, I do. To tell you the truth, uncle, I don't care a bit what anybody ever did."

The skilled mechanic or artisan of to-day certainly has little occasion to care what anybody ever did in ancient Greece or Rome, since his daily occupation brings him in contact with such marvels of applied science that the past tends to seem insignificant.

The growing respect for eastern, and particularly Indian ideas, which I suppose in the main dates from Max Müller's edition of the *Sacred Books of the East*, and which has increased since the peace of 1919 with the publication of Sir Charles Eliot's great work on Hinduism and Buddhism and the *exposé* of Indian philosophy by Prof. Rada-krishnan, has still further promoted western interest in pantheistic modes of thought. The Ganges is flowing into the Thames, and (even greater extravagance) into the Mississippi. The results may be seen in various popular movements. So called Christian Science, whatever its practical expression, is based upon the axiom "All is God, all is good, evil is an illusion." (6) The popularity of theosophical movements may be partly traceable to the same type of doctrine. It is said that the remarkable success of the posthumous publication of Rolt's translation of the pseudo-Dionysian writings in 1920 (7) was due to the avidity with which it was taken up by English theosophists, since these writings are (as is well known) extremely sympathetic in their treatment of certain Indian teachings which influenced Plotinus as the result of his sojourn in the Punjab.

The immense popularity of the works of Mr Ralph Waldo Trine (8) is another instance of the loose pantheistic tendencies of the day. Mr Trine is by training an American journalist, and his books, which are very numerous, have grave literary blemishes; but they are to be found on sale in the vast majority of English and American bookshops. His essay *In Tune with the Infinite* has had a circulation of over 831,000 copies, and has passed through 21 American editions. It is obvious therefore that its influence has been very wide. A few specimens of the best part of his teaching may be given. "We differ from God in that we are individualised spirits, while He is the infinite spirit including us as well as all else beside, yet in essence the life of God and the life of man are identically the same and so are one."

"We are always divine, but that divinity is latent."

After speaking of the divine life and human life as resembling reservoirs of water, great and small, in which the smaller is fed by the greater, he proceeds:

"Whatever difference exists is a difference of degree; in quality they are identical."

The logic of facts leads him at this point into an inconsistency which he appears to ignore since he recognises that the individual is capable of resisting the inflow of the divine substance. It appears, therefore, that the human will is invested somehow with a kind of independence or separateness. He continues: "The God-life, Divine being, is the one life, and there is no life that is apart from it.... Round and round within a wheel roams the vagrant

soul so long as it fancies itself different and apart
from the supreme. It becomes truly immortal when
upheld by Him."

He quotes the old couplet:

> Know this, O man, sole root of sin in thee
> Is not to know thy own divinity,

and also the saying of Paracelsus:

> The only death to be feared is separation from the life of God.

This kind of teaching, though much of it is shallow,
illogical, and full of inconsistencies, is plainly an
honest attempt at popularising eastern ideas among
the masses in the West. It regards Christ as the
supreme instance of a nature-mystic, and His
teaching and example as the finest object-lesson of
the way in which to live in tune with the Infinite,
and it must be admitted that there is much good
in such a view, so far as it goes: but of course it
is fundamentally separated from the ordinary
western presentation of Christianity, with its promise of an individual immortality.

It seems probable that on the latter point there
is considerable vagueness of belief among Protestant
Christians to-day. Not long since I encountered in a
certain Y.M.C.A. magazine a poem, published apparently with the approval of a Christian editor, in
which the following occurred (I should explain that
the writer pictures himself in a great temple, a
kind of mixture of a Christian cathedral and
Zoroastrian fire-temple):

> I saw the white robed priests
> Bend down in humble worship

Before a giant flame
That filled the building.

. . . .

In my dreams I spake saying,
"Why worship ye a flame?"
And lo the singing ceased.
Up rose the white robed priests,
And the flame grew brighter,
Until it kissed the roof above.
"We worship the flame of Life,
This great fire that thou seest,
Created in the beginning
By the omnipotent God,
Will burn for all eternity;
For it is fed by the flames of men."

. . . .

I thought of how like a flame
Our short life is.
A flame that flickers softly and joyously
When we are young and happy,
And how in later youth
It rises to its greatest height,
Then flickers low once more,
As dull care and age creep on
Till this poor body dies.
Sending its flame to that great temple
There to join the flame of universal and eternal life,
That is fed by the flames of men.

I am far from wishing to exaggerate the merits
of this effusion, but I think it is a fair specimen of
the way in which a species of pantheism is finding
popular expression.

I will venture upon one more quotation from a
totally different source, the writings of a well known
Anglo-American professor (9). In his *Stewardship of
Faith*, at the conclusion of the chapter upon
Gnosticism he writes: "The question will be raised
...whether we may not be mistaken in thinking
that the difference between 'you' and 'me' is so

very important. Suppose that that is only the limitation of life, not the expression of it; that what happens after death is that the life which has been as it were bottled up in our individualities is released, and goes back into the main stream. That is also a survival of life after death. We have no right even to say that in that case it does not matter what we do with our own little bit of life. It *does* matter, because we are affecting the main stream after we return to it." Something of the same spirit may be found in an essay on Immortality written by Dean Inge a few years ago (10).

In Germany there is a marked increase in interest in eastern modes of religious thought. A typical instance of this is to be found in the activities of Graf Herrmann von Keyserling (11). This nobleman set himself at the end of the war to make a tour of the East, in order to acquaint himself at first hand with its ideas. He kept a very full diary which he has since published, and the balance of his opinion seems to lie in favour of philosophic Buddhism, for the promotion of which he has inaugurated a community in his native land. A literature of this neo-Buddhism has developed, and Steffen (12) gives five reasons for its popularity.

1. It puts forward the claim to be scientific.

2. It claims to supersede the materialistic monism of the continent as an atheistic religion without belief in a soul and with respect for the aesthetic values of pessimism.

3. By its denial on principle of all dogma it gives free play for speculation.

4. By being free from history and personality it can successfully oppose the individualistic tendencies of the day.

5. In spite of the pessimism of its world view it has an optimistic view of life, and a lofty ethic which is favourable to culture.

In the 1923 issue of the *Zeitschrift für Theologie und Kirche*, a learned periodical which formerly devoted itself to New Testament, Patristics, Christian Doctrine, and the like, four of the longest articles (out of a total of nineteen) deal with some aspect or other of mysticism or oriental pantheism; the first with occultism and theosophy, the fifth by Kattenbusch concerning the distinction between experiencing God and believing in God, the eighth describing the Zen sect of Japanese Buddhists, and the thirteenth Keyserling's philosophy of religion.

It must finally be noted that the real strength of Islam to-day, apart from its creation of an international brotherhood, lies not in its moral code or detailed system of doctrine so much as in its deterministic theology. Islam means submission, submission to the all-prevailing will of God. The individual is thus reduced to a nullity in order that the will of God may prevail. It is not surprising that the most vital elements in living Islam are mystical movements. Pantheistic sufism is no recent growth, as a glance at Prof. Nicholson's book will show (13), but in its doctrine of the Perfect Man supplies a fresh element in the pantheistic conception of the universe. The Perfect Man, like George Fox the Quaker, is one who lives in harmony or unity with the creation, and is therefore the visible completion of the Divine idea.

I desire to speak with all possible sympathy of these vast systems of religious sentiment and thought. They are only equalled in extent and complexity by those which have gathered themselves round the teaching of Christ, and no sane person can afford to treat them with negligence or contempt. There is an obvious borderland between the two groups in which the Christian and non-Christian mystics mingle and often seem to speak the same language, and the modern interest in mysticism is itself a proof of the tendency to adopt quasi-pantheistic views of life and to stress to its utmost limits the doctrine of divine immanence contained in the text "in Him we live and move and have our being."

"I understood," says St Teresa, "how our Lord was in all things and how He was in the soul, and the simile of a saturated sponge was suggested to me." (14) This is not very far from the view of Mr Trine. The opposite to it is of course the theory of emanations, as in Aquinas, Dionysius the Areopagite and the Kabbalists; and such a theory of present emanations is of course not incompatible with belief in an ultimate pantheism or panentheism.

Perhaps at this point we should pause to make a brief note of the two main streams of modern philosophy, as they bear upon the problem before us. On the one hand, we have from Spinoza to Bradley, in the recognition of the One rather than the Many, an attempt to work out the true idea of the universe as a significant whole. On the other hand, we have the opposite tendency, from Leibnitz to Ward, to emphasise the Many at the expense of the One. Both, it will be observed, find their natural difficulty in regard to the nature of the Absolute, i.e. all that is. To Bradley a personal God is not the ultimate truth of the universe, yet a personal God is more real than you or me. But the status of such a God is only relative, and both His status and ours are insecure. We are all in danger of being at any moment withdrawn into and lost in the Absolute. To James God is not the name of the whole of things but only of the ideal tendency in things, believed in as a superhuman person who calls us to co-operate in His purpose....He works in an external environment, has limits, and has enemies....If the Absolute exists in addition, the Absolute is only the wider "cosmic" whole of which our God is but the most ideal portion. The pluralistic world is thus more like a federal republic than like an empire or kingdom. But this single God of James is really the same as the many Gods of Buddhist philosophy —a finite being. What of the rest of what there is? And what is the relation of God and ourselves to that rest? Is the ultimate existence the whole in-clusive system—the impersonal universe? Can we speak of God, or use the word Theist when our Theos is neither personal, nor moral, but only ultimate? Is it not more correct under such cir-cumstances to call ourselves pantheists and to worship the all-inclusive universe, impersonal but ultimate, of which we ourselves are but temporary kinks or discontinuities? (15)

The root problem of pantheism lies in its conception of the course of events. As we Christians look at it we seem to see a procession of individual and self-determining beings. The thorough-going pantheist says that this apparent self-determination is an illusion. God is everything, and all that exists in time is simply a temporary phase of complexity in His being. One type of Indian thought calls it the sport of God, as it were the expenditure of His surplus energy. History is only like the crumpling of a flat sheet of paper. This adds nothing to the area of the paper, nor does it construct a shape which possesses any permanency; God can, and does, and will again and again smooth out the creases and all shall be as before. In this system there is plenty of room for gods many and lords many, since even the highest personal god is simply the highest created being. The whole world as *we* see and experience it is nothing but an imperfect appearance of pure being, imperfect because it is a cycle of coming into existence and ceasing, of ceasing and coming into existence; imperfect also because of the struggle and conflict among individuals occasioned by the will to live. The real deity in this case is, as Professor Pratt observes, the universe of pure being which is, he says, "an exceedingly pragmatic deity." [16] The worship of such a deity simply consists in obeying the laws of the universe, and such a conclusion is arrived at by many Chinese philosophers, although by quite a different route.

It is impossible not to respect the earnest efforts of these seekers of the East after a unified system

of thought and worship. Yet it is equally impossible
to feel satisfied with the results. A system which
denies freedom to the individual in the direction of
God delivers a blow at the finest part of the moral
life. Moreover, whether the individual be ultimate
or no (a question to which we shall attend presently)
his sense of being at present separate is a fact of
life which cannot be explained away. Either sin is
a reality or there is no such thing as the distinction
between moral good and evil. If God is everything
which is, then he obviously includes within Himself
Patrick Mahon and all his misdeeds as well as the
holiness of all the saints.

It soon follows from this that the logical issue of
pantheism is pessimism. It is only because Mr Trine
is not a profound thinker but a journalist that he
is able to be cheerful and obsessed with optimism.
He is a typical specimen of the person who instead
of going to college chapel on a fine Sunday goes out
"to discover God in nature." The objection to this
priggish explanation of a very innocent and widespread custom is that nature consists also of bad
weather, and that if God is in nature rather than
at mattins then He is equally in the rainstorm and
the cutting north-east wind, and we should go out
to find Him quite as much under uncomfortable as
under pleasant circumstances. Whether we consider pantheism in East or West, its dominating
tendency so far as it is consistent is pessimistic.
Nothing has any real value. The identification of
everything that *is* with God if thoroughly and con-
sistently undertaken must inevitably blur distinc-

tions, and lead to the supposition that the good and the beautiful cannot be so good and beautiful as they seem, or that the evil and loathsome have a beauty of their own which one can be trained to appreciate. But this soon involves us in the decadence of a Baudelaire.

Prof. Urquhart(17) defines a normal system of thought as one which takes account of the whole of ordinary human experience, and he points out that one chief inadequacy of pantheism is its abnormality. He has several further objections which are so clearly put that I think I cannot do better than discuss them in order. Pantheism, he points out, is a system of unstable equilibrium. The slightest pressure in the direction either of logical consistency or simple experience causes the balance between subject and object to topple over one way or the other. "Rigorous application of principles compels us to identify God with the whole world or with none of it. The choice of the former lands us in the dilemma of choosing again between acosmism (God is all), or the identification of the world in every detail with God."(18) Abstract pantheism seems attractive when it tells us that ordinary experience is a dream. Thus Mrs Eddy although she disdains pantheism, says, in harmony with many pantheists proper, "Life in matter is a dream. Sin, sickness and death are this dream. Life is Spirit, and when we waken from the dream of life in matter, we shall learn this grand truth of being."(19) This is a delightfully easy way of escape from trouble, and it may be useful in dealing with patients who are suffering from diseases of the nervous system. But all difficulties and evils of life are not dreams. We find it impossible to wake up out of them. If they are illusions then it follows that illusion forms the major part of our daily reality. "We find ourselves still in the prison house, and our gloom is deeper than before, because we have dreamed of freedom and awakened to find that it is only a dream."

Pantheism promises identity with the One and Absolute; but if this identity already exists, why is it necessary to promise it? Who makes the promise, and to whom is it made? The abnormal nature of the system again manifests itself in the inability to give a proper answer to such questions. There is neither consistency nor attractiveness about the Indian gentleman who declared to Prof. Hopkins: "I, being completely developed, worship myself, my wife, being incompletely developed, worships bare image." (20) This is of course only an absurd instance of a quite serious phenomenon in metaphysical mysticism of an extreme kind. The *Theologia Germanica* speaks of deification and of the "vergöttete Mensch"; but deification, as Mrs Stuart Moore observes, is not in this case a scientific term.

Pantheism promises us, as has been said, identity with the One and Absolute; but it is an identity of absorption, and absorption in something which is unknown. It has been described as the peace which passeth understanding, but as Prof. Urquhart says, "Although it may pass understanding it is hardly peace, unless that is peace which consists in shutting the eyes to difficulties."

Pantheism creates in us a profound sense of intellectual discouragement. The unity of the pantheist with the permanent reality which lies beyond phenomena (although described by Mr Allanson Picton as an intenser unity than any we know) is really a unity in which all distinctions are lost, not one in which they are conserved and explained. The unwarrantable assumption is made that a state of being in which there are no differentiations at all must have a higher absolute value than a rich complexity. The fact is we cannot for ever disregard the problems of our finite experience, and the result follows that pantheism inevitably produces either scepticism or extravagance. This is the reason for the transition in India from pantheism to polytheism, and in mediaeval Europe from mysticism to sheer idolatry. It is not accidental that many great Catholic mystics exist side by side with an extravagant eucharistic devotion and an extravagant cultus of the saints. Moreover, the insistence upon the unknowable character of ultimate reality is likely to have a damaging effect upon the construction of scientific theory, while on the emotional side this view of life leads undoubtedly to an evaporation of interest and ideals.

If we look at the other extreme into which pantheism falls when it is disturbed from its position of unstable equilibrium, it is fairly obvious that emphasis on the first syllable (pan) soon lands us in a world from which God has disappeared. The monism of the man of science of twenty years ago is as unsatisfying as the acosmism of the Indian thinker. It is also equally abnormal. The facts of

the world as stated by this system do not correspond
to our normal human cravings. I quote from the
monist catechism. "There being no room for a
moral order in the physical and chemical constitu-
tion of the universe and in the history of the
organic world existing for countless years, there are
no other laws prevailing in the history of nations
than the all-dominant precepts of nature." This
kind of doctrine brings us back to the secularism
of the bolshevik, and it is not surprising to read in
the next sentence of the catechism: "The struggle
for existence is not fought out and decided by the
moral order, but by the physical and intellectual
excellence, activity and superiority of the individual." (21) The treatment of evil, suffering, and
freedom is equally unsatisfactory in view of normal
human instincts. Pantheism is bound to lead to
determinism; both Stoics and the Indian philosophers as well as a number of modern scientists
treat the individual as a helpless detail in a con-
tinuous process. It is, as Prof. Urquhart remarks,
to a certain extent comforting to know that everything is done for us and that we do not need to
trouble ourselves: but supposing things go wrong,
are we prepared to put up with it? Are we content
to say with Marcus Aurelius (22): "Since matter,
motion, and mortals are in a perpetual flux...I
cannot imagine what there is here that is worth
minding or being eager about. On the other hand
a man ought to keep up his spirits, for it will not
be long before his discharge comes." This is all very
well, but the philosophic Emperor soon passes on

to the glorification of suicide, and to suggestions about giving life the slip (23). "If the room smokes, leave it." It requires very little power of perception to see that the Christian view is infinitely superior which makes life a game to be played to the end and won. Although it is generally regarded as an item to the credit of the Buddha that he discouraged suicide and taught that it involved re-birth under less favourable circumstances, the reply must be made that he substituted for it—the cloister.

To avoid confusion, I think it is only fair to dis-tinguish between those who treat pantheism as a theory of present existence which truly describes the condition of all objects animate and inanimate as it really is, and those who regard pantheism or at least panentheism in some form or other as the goal towards which the whole universe is moving. Many will feel that the objections which have been urged against the former do not apply to the latter. They will say that the differentiation of which we are all conscious is actual and not illusory, but they will quote St Paul's text about all things being subdued until God is all in all as evidence that from apostolic times Christians have been able with-out inconsistency to hold a pantheistic view of the future (24). They will also quote in support the text from the fourth gospel in which Christ is represented as praying, "I in them, and thou in me that they may all be one even as we are one." (25) It is very doubtful whether the texts so quoted are meant to be taken *au pied de la lettre*, as cold prose—actual mathematical descriptions of the fate of the indi-

vidual. It seems much more likely that they are to
be understood in the same way as the sentiments
of certain hymns:

> Now let me gain perfection's height
> Now let me into nothing fall:
> Be less than nothing in my sight
> And feel that Christ is all in all. (26)

Or

> Till in the ocean of thy love
> We lose ourselves in heaven above. (27)

Or again

> Till we cast our crowns before Thee,
> Lost in wonder, love and praise. (28)

Self-forgetfulness is not the same as self-extinction.
There is no need to go further than Walter Hilton:
"Perfect love maketh God and the soul to be as if
they both together were but one thing," (29) or
St Bernard: "When I love God with my will I transform myself unto Him, for it is the power or virtue
of love that it maketh Thee to be like unto that
which thou lovest." (30) There is perhaps little to be
gained from discussing the nature of a future state
of existence of the details of which we can have no
real information, and there will be not a few who
will like to content themselves with the guarded
confession of Prof. Lake to which I have previously
referred. I venture to suggest however that we have
a right to ask at least one thing about the future.
It is certainly a normal human craving to have some
assurance that the spiritual nucleus which we call
the individual soul really has a future in store for
it. It seems to many of us a waste of time for the
Creator Spirit to bring individual souls into existence

and to spend infinite pains on their education, if in the end they are simply to be re-absorbed into the Divine Essence. The process reminds us of a child playing with plasticine, or building sand castles on the sea-shore. In fact, as Sankara candidly says: "The activity of the Lord may be supposed to be mere sport, proceeding from His own nature without reference to any purpose." (31) It is a matter of considerable interest that this sort of thought has given way in some Indian schools of philosophy to the system of Ramanuja, which is a qualified monism. Ramanuja taught that Brahman is not without attributes but is possessed of all imaginable good qualities. Nothing exists apart from him and both matter and souls are merely modes of his existence. He emits the world and individual souls by an act of volition, and the souls begin the process of transmigration. Salvation is obtained by right knowledge and meditation aided by the grace of God. The soul released from the wheel of life is not absorbed in God or identified with Him but enjoys a blissful, personal existence, and shares in His glorious qualities. This is more like European theism than many of the creeds of India, but even Ramanuja, though he did not believe the world to be an illusion, described the highest god as one who "in sport produces, sustains, and re-absorbs the entire universe, and whose only aim is to foster the manifold classes of beings that humbly worship him."

The conclusion which I wish to draw is that these very strict and rigid systems of philosophy shatter themselves upon the rocks of normal human desire.

The purest form of Buddhism died in the country of its origin, and survives chiefly in the cloisters of Ceylon. Buddhism, in fact, has only been able to expand by adopting the personal saviour and the personal heaven, and it is well known that popular Cingalese Buddhism is extremely animistic. The greatest weakness of pantheism is its inability to think nobly of the soul of the common man. Thus it is said of the lofty principles of Spinoza: "The main difficulty in accepting his teaching is that it is an ethic for philosophers alone. It neglects the common man, it provides no way of making him a man worth saving." [32] There is no good news for the poor, the mourner, or the oppressed: pantheism has no permanently troubled social conscience, and can never lift the burden of the world's pain.

But there is a further objection to pantheism of a totally different sort, i.e. that it makes a clean sweep of the whole of historical science. To the pantheist nothing significant ever really happens. The attributes of God are eternal and unchanging, and the character of the Absolute, if indeed the Absolute can be said to possess character at all, is unchanging, while the cycle of events is either sport or illusion. Now whatever we may have to say in succeeding lectures about the value of historical Christianity over other forms of theism, at least it is reasonable to assert that the respect for history which is the distinctive feature of the Judaeo-Christian complex renders the latter far superior to any system in which the whole of historical science is ignored. History after all must be taken into account; it does add something to the data of philosophy. As an English writer in the *Monist* (33) has pointed out, it introduces what Bertrand Russell calls mnemic causation and also insists upon the uniqueness both of events and of persons. History gives in addition the characteristics of mnemic causality and mind or thought in general, e.g. the processes and products of the arts which are certainly parts of the real world, and are social things, realities which can only be understood in reference to a plurality of minds. This uniqueness is a fundamental fact, and history *never* repeats itself. I do not wish to recapitulate all that was said on this point some ten years ago by a distinguished member of our divinity faculty, but will confine myself to a quotation or two from his essay: "Our Christian notion is that Reality is one unique performance of a great stage play never repeated, not an immovable group of statues which can be looked at from various points of view but which never itself changes; and what is more, God Himself is one of the actors" . . . . "The death of our Lord on the cross (for instance) is understood by Christians to have changed the relations between God and man" . . . "When we try to look at things *sub specie aeternitatis* it still remains a real Event." (34) In other words, the Christian religion champions the essential reality and uniqueness of all events, and the reality of time.

And one more objection. The pantheistic systems, whether in East or West, are, I admit, logical. But they are only so by sacrificing the desire for recognition of the highest human values. Schweitzer

points out (35) that if it is a case of constructing a
tidy explanation of the world the religious philosophies of nature, whether they be speculative
German philosophies, or those of the Stoics, or that
of Spinoza, or the systems of the Far East, as systems
are unassailable. But religion has not only to explain the world; it has also to answer the need that
we feel for giving a purpose to our lives. Logical
thought about the nature of the universe cannot
reach an ethic. Every reasonable religion has to
choose between these two alternatives, and we
Christians are not afraid of contradiction when we
assert that ours is the better choice. The knowledge
we derive from the experience of God as ethical
will is more vital than the knowledge derived from
nature. The knowledge derived from nature re-
sembles the knowledge derived from a map of an
area of country. It reduces it to a system, classifies
it, and enables the traveller to find his way about.
But it does not exhaustively explain its significance
from every point of view. The knowledge of God as
ethical will is derived, so we say, from conscience
and from history. Both stand on the same side.
Thus we declare that the true character of God is
displayed in the course of events which centres
round the crucifixion of Jesus Christ, and which
reveals the universe as controlled by a loving,
suffering, and self-limiting God.

I seem to have spent so much time in criticising the
pantheistic interpretation of life that some may feel
that I have underrated its attractiveness. In defence
let me say that I have purposely put down all the

objections at length. I freely recognise that many
of my fellow men have chosen to adopt some sort
of pantheistic mysticism in a spirit of real earnestness. Almost every modern tendency encourages
them to do this. The critical study of the Bible
prejudices them against a religion based upon proof-
texts. The study of the natural sciences encourages
them to look for God everywhere or nowhere, and
to discover Him in nature rather than in interven-
tions or interruptions of the natural law. To those
who are but imperfectly acquainted with Christianity
the eastern systems present many charming features.
The advantages of theosophy, for example, are to be
found not in its jargon or ridiculous cosmogony so
much as in the rules it gives for bringing oneself into
certain exalted states of consciousness, which not
only produce happiness but also a serene temper
which is pleasant to one's neighbours. But my
answer to all this is that all these benefits can be
obtained in the Christian religion without recourse to
theosophy or indeed any kind of oriental mysticism,
while to adopt a genuinely pantheistic interpretation of the universe must in the end land the consistent thinker in a slough of melancholy difficulties.
While recognising therefore that my friends are
actuated by honest religious motives, I wish to
warn them against following what seems certain to
prove a blind alley.

Let me summarise as briefly as I can the reason
why Christian theism seems a so much richer and
more satisfying alternative.

First of all, it satisfies the moral conscience. The

latter urges us to think of God as possessing moral
qualities. Now we cannot think of morality except
as the characteristic of a being who is at least
personal. Personality is our most valuable possession and we cannot think of the ultimately valuable
in terms of something which is less than the highest
value we know. Even in the East, Tulsidas expresses
the discontent of multitudes when he says: "The
worship of the impersonal laid no hold upon my
heart." (36) Deity which is super-personal need not
be the same as Deity which is impersonal, although
the two are often spoken of as though they were
identical.

In the second place it is impossible, whatever may
be the opinion in certain sophisticated circles, to
conceive that differentiated existence is an inferior,
if not an evil thing. It must be borne in mind that
some philosophers are so profoundly convinced of
the essential worth of the individual that they declare that reality consists only in a plurality of
souls. The Christian religion affirms that life eternal
consists in knowing God, not in being absorbed in
Him, and that Jesus Christ came to promise more
life and not less life to men. We are not content
that our loved ones should disappear in the abyss
of an impersonal deity. Francis Thompson can
hardly be said to have found life easy, and might
have welcomed the peace of utter extinction, yet in
his essay on Shelley he proudly disdains it. Com-
menting on Shelley's lines:

> He is a portion of that loveliness
> Which once he made more lovely...

he says:

"What utter desolation can it be that discerns comfort in this hope, whose wan countenance is the countenance of a despair!...What deepest depths of agony is it that finds consolation in this immortality, an immortality which thrusts you into death, the maw of nature, that your dissolved elements may circulate through her veins....Better almost the black resignation which the fatalist draws from his own hopelessness." (37)

This is the true Christian fortitude based upon the gospel of Calvary. Henley gets very near to it when he says: "I thank whatever Gods may be, for my unconquerable soul"—(I do not think it is very kind to suggest that he is merely suffering from an inferiority-complex).

It is strange how nervous some theologians are about describing God as a person and making personal immortality an integral part of Christian doctrine. The standing instance of course is Schleiermacher, and in modern times we see the same tendency in Troeltsch, who in fact shows very strong traces of Schleiermacher's influence. Some of our Anglicans however tend to become equally nebulous. Their intention is good enough. They want to secure the doctrines in question from all childish anthropomorphic limitations, but they end in a quasi-pantheism. It is all very well to say that it is not we but only our ideals and our values that matter. It has been pointed out (38) that we are not the temporary bearers of values like money in our pockets. We are these values. They are personal values, the genuine choices of free personality, and both must surely be thought of as existing inseparably together. It is no more uncomfortable to believe in a unity of the human soul with God as distinct from absorption, than to think of the union of the sulphur and hydrogen atoms in a drop of acid which is yet no absorption of either, since they are capable of being separated. The goal is a rich complexity, and not a blank absence of differentiation.

And then, in the fourth place, the Christian does not regard the world as the mere play of God's fancy. He believes that God has of serious purpose limited Himself of His own free will by bringing into existence a number of creative beings, self-conscious centres of initiative, having freedom of action and self-determination. God for love's sake has made Himself finite. This reality of human individual activity gives a genuine value to human history. It has often been noticed how indifferent India has been to her past history. India hardly troubles to record the names of great men who have made her what she is. Man is just a part of nature, not the lord of nature. Similarly the art of India does not deal in portraits, but represents man as part of the surrounding landscape. The thought of history as a real sequence and of God as manifesting Himself through individuals in the time-process is almost as foreign to the mathematician and pure scientist as to the Indian philosopher. Yet a scientific *Weltanschauung* which omits to take account of history is obviously incomplete. In my fourth lecture I hope to try to say something constructive about the contribution of historical science to the estimate of the Christian religion, but for the moment I will simply point out that the Christian claims that there *is* a purpose in history, and that God is *inside* the temporal process.

There is for me no small satisfaction in finding that one who quite whole-heartedly professes to be a Christian, after a much closer first-hand acquaintance with non-Christian systems than I possess, should be able to express so clearly the conclusion which I, working independently in a much narrower and totally different environment, have also reached but do not feel able to express nearly so well. Prof. Urquhart (39), writing from Calcutta and insisting on the wonders of the universe suggests that eternity is a mode in which we express value. "Although the home of value is really in a realm raised above the temporal process, the latter has its contribution to make to that realm. We need not insist that the temporal process should be at any given moment completed before we can speak of Absolute Value. If then we identify God with Absolute Value, we do not diminish that value by thinking of temporal process as not yet completed, even for God. . . . We may without irreverence think of God as Himself evolving, differentiating Himself according to the laws of organic growth, but with far greater specification. . . . We may regard God as entering into the world of time through the creation of human personalities, whose freedom He will not retract. . . . The end will be the Kingdom of God, the realm of the completely triumphant spiritual, and into this kingdom we shall bring all that we have truly won in the temporal struggle, and shall find our places as free personalities, each one of us discovering in the Kingdom of God the Kingdom of His own Spirit." (40)

Last of all, Christian mysticism is a moral mysticism, and in no way comparable with a non-moral and often immoral nature-mysticism. It recognises the existence of sin and the need of the purgative way. It calls for renunciation, faith, and obedience, and the putting away of fleshly appetites and a self-regarding complacency. Before we can say "All things are ours and we are Christ's and Christ's is God's" we must have crucified the old man: and that is often the work of a life-time.

LECTURE III

TRADITIONALISM

IT is not very easy to find a really good name for the third system which offers itself as an alternative to vital Christianity. I have ventured to call it "traditionalism," but confess that I am not entirely satisfied with the word. Anyhow it is a fairly convenient description of what I have in mind.

If we take a general view of the world, we observe that Christians are roughly divided into three groups —definite Catholics, definite Protestants, and lying between the two a number of moderate reformed churches of which the Anglican communion is the largest. By "definite Catholic" I mean to include both Rome and the eastern churches, as well as some of those Anglicans who agree in the main with them. By "definite Protestant" I mean to include all who have abandoned completely the idea of a sacrificial ministry and the necessity of any sacrament, and who hold themselves little if at all bound by the chains of past tradition. Now it must be plain to any unprejudiced student of church history that the expression of the Christian religion has reached what is commonly called the Catholic position in the following way. All over the world distributed more or less uniformly is a large mass of traditional faith and practice which is of extreme antiquity, and which on investigation seems to cohere, in spite of individual nuances and national and local customs. Bishop Gore once called it(1) the real natural religion of humanity, as distinct from the so-called natural religion of the eighteenth century theorists. There is no need for our purposes to force a decision on the doubtful issue of its origin, since we are still not in possession of sufficient data to be able to say whether it all sprang from one source or cradle, or whether the human intelligence, observing the same kind of natural phenomena independently at different points on the earth's surface, drew similar inferences, and led by common instincts built up a series of independent cults, having many features in common. The final product has the same look about it, whatever its origin.

Now any prophetic religion, founded by the personal efforts of an inspired individual, has always had to reckon with this extraordinary pluralistic network, and it has seldom been able to escape the necessity of coming to terms with it. The most familiar example I can think of is that to be found recorded in the literature of the Old Testament. Here we have the spectacle of a pure and spiritual monotheism opposing itself to a traditional polytheistic cultus. Most, though not all of the prophets are Puritan iconoclasts, and their policy if adopted meant a complete breach with the existing popular practice. It appears however that many other Hebrews were perfectly willing to make a treaty with the nature religions, and not only to maintain a central temple where a variety of sacrificial rites was performed, but even to tolerate the existence of a number of local high-places, where ceremonies were enacted of a more or less idolatrous character.

We get the spectacle of the same kind of thing in India where the extremely rarified and abstract tenets of the higher Hinduism do not exclude a tolerance of the grossest polytheistic rites which amazes the observer. Islam from the first set its face firmly against any sort of treaty with the traditional cultus, but even in this case a good deal of animistic superstition has managed to creep in.

The Christian religion, emerging as it did from the pure prophetic faith of Israel, was forced to encounter the same dilemma. As displayed in the person of its founder it is more completely free from emphasis upon institutional observances than any other religion, Islam not excepted. There is no certain evidence that Jesus Christ during His earthly ministry ordained anything like what the church of succeeding ages has chosen to call the sacramental system, although Christians have certainly believed that in holding together the fellowship of believers by some social ordinances they have acted under the direct guidance of the spirit of the living Jesus and have received His blessing. Christian discipleship however in its purest form has demanded so high a moral and spiritual standard that I fear we must honestly admit that it could not in so short a time have become the popular and widespread religion that it has, if many of its propagators had not suffered themselves to enter into a treaty with the traditional religions of the races of mankind. From the moment that Christianity moved out of purely Jewish surroundings it began to make terms with the religious practices of the Graeco-Roman

and Middle Eastern worlds. The history of this
process is obscure, because we do not know the
actual steps by which it advanced. We do not know
for example to what extent St Paul when he uses
the language of the mystery-religions means it to
be taken seriously, and of course he is all the time
a loyal Hebrew in his resistance to idolatry and to
the recognition of daemons. At any rate the general
structure of the worship and organisation of the
Church in Europe after apostolic times proceeded
upon the lines of syncretism. So much at least may
be regarded as established beyond dispute. It is
useless to produce the writings of a limited number
of educated churchmen during the first five centuries, and to argue from them that the Christian
religion remained uninfluenced by its pagan environment. The real test must be, "What is the
evidence of popular practice?" and this evidence
points conclusively as we know in the direction of
compromise. As Dean Inge(2) has put it: "The
nomina were changed, the numina remained the
same." Most of the typical accompaniments of
organised worship on the continent are derived from
pre-Christian worship, such as was associated, for example, with the cult of the Alexandrian divinity Isis.
The tendency to adore a projection of the mother-
complex is world-wide, and where the personality
of God is not strongly felt to include the attributes
of both sexes, mankind is almost certain to set up
the worship of the most mighty Mother. Hence the
transference to Mary the Mother of Christ of much
devotion which might otherwise have been offered

to Him. Of Easter, Bede frankly says(3), "people now call the Paschal time after the goddess Eostre, giving a name to the new festal solemnities from the accustomed vocabulary of ancient rites and ob-servances" (*consueto antiquae observationis vocabulo gaudia novae solemnitatis vocantes*). It is well known that many saints of the Roman calendar are not really historical characters but transformations of mythical personages whose cultus preceded the arrival of the Christian Church. Just such mythical personages are the St George of the dragon episode, St Catherine of the wheel, and almost certainly St Christopher, whose veneration is apparently the best kind of devotion that Rome feels able to offer for the Parisian motor mechanic. At Eleusis a church of St Demetrius was erected on the site of a temple of Demeter. St Cosmas and St Damian, whatever their historical origin, draw to themselves the cultus of the Dioscuri. A recent work by a retired missionary bishop(4) on "the village gods of South India" points out that these deities, as repre-senting the fertile pro-creative element in nature, are mostly of the female sex. But it is not to India alone that such conceptions are limited. There is no other equally satisfactory explanation of the extra-ordinary prevalence and popularity throughout un-reformed Christianity of the local or village Madonna. The exposition of the doctrine of Holy Communion by the Roman Catholic Bishop of Newport, (3) a book which apparently finds favour among certain Anglicans, is based not merely upon a naïve inter-pretation of Scripture which will not admit of scrutiny, but upon an acceptance of such views of the use of the Blessed Sacrament as are obviously derived from paganism in its impact upon the infant Christian Church, although they are undoubtedly in harmony with much patristic evidence. Perhaps the most violent instance of an extreme piece of syncretism is the form of sacrificing a fowl with Christian prayers which occurs among the offices of one of the lesser eastern Churches.

These are but a few instances drawn from a vast mass of evidence which cannot possibly be given at length in one brief lecture: but I defy anyone to refute the conclusions which are drawn from it. The whole of Latin Christianity to-day both in countries where it has long been established, and also in the mission field, as well as the Christianity of Russia and that of the Churches of the Near and Middle East —all this represents a policy of compromise with the traditional religious systems which preceded the coming of the gospel. I am not denying for the moment that this policy is incapable of defence: as is well known, Fr Tyrrell and others have defended it on pragmatic grounds. But I think it is important that it should be called by its proper name. It is frankly an experiment at creating a world religion by grafting what is admitted on all hands to be the purest spiritual religion which has ever appeared on this planet on to previously existing religious systems in order to disturb them as little as possible. I admit that it is rather a lengthy experiment, but if we bear in mind the age of the earth I do not see that it is deserving of a better name. Measured by certain standards it may claim to have been a successful experiment, and the lessons of the modern mission field teach us that it is not wise to dismiss it entirely with a gesture of contempt. The question of the extent to which people newly converted to discipleship may be allowed to keep some at any rate of their old customs crops up again and again, and it occurred in the early history of our own Church, as may be seen from Augustine's correspondence with Pope Gregory, whose replies to questions seem to indicate a statement of official policy. Thus in a letter of Gregory's quoted by Bede[5], that Pope, after giving orders that the pagan temples were on no account to be destroyed, but to be cleansed and hallowed for Christian worship, proceeds: "As they have been wont to hold sacrificial feasts, it will be wise to provide them with some other enjoyments by way of compensation. On the day of the dedication, or on the festivals of those saints whose relics are there deposited, let the converts make themselves 'tabernacles' with boughs of trees around the temples now turned into churches, and there kill oxen, no longer in sacrifice to devils, but as the materials of their meal, and with thanks to the Giver of all things." For, he says: "you cannot cut off everything at once from rough natures: he who would climb to a height must ascend step by step, he cannot jump the whole way." Father Delehaye[6] says frankly: "In point of fact it would be very surprising if when seeking to propagate her doctrines in the midst of Graeco-Roman civilisation the Church had adopted for her

intercourse with the people a wholly unknown
language, and had systematically repudiated everything that until then had served to give expression
to religious feeling....It was natural that the new
religion should end by appropriating to itself a whole
ritual which only required to be sanely interpreted
to become the language of the Christian soul aspiring
to the one True God. All external signs which did
not implicitly involve the recognition of polytheism
would find grace in the eyes of the Church; and if
on the one hand she showed no undue haste in
adopting them officially to her use, on the other
hand she did not protest when they made their
appearance as a means of expressing the religious
instincts of the people"; and again: "If we are told
that the ideas disseminated through society by hero
worship predisposed the mind to a ready acceptance
of the rôle of saints in the Christian dispensation,
and of their value as intercessors before God, I see
no reason whatever for contesting the statement."
There will be few experienced missionaries who have
not, in facing the question, compromised where such
compromise seemed to involve no betrayal of
principle. It is quite easy to stress the insistence
upon the uniqueness of Christianity to such an
extent as to depreciate unduly the amount of truth
and beauty which in a fragmentary state exist in
many pagan faiths, or are symbolically expressed in
their customs, and in any case our anthropologist
friends are never tired of pointing out to us the
extreme peril of too hasty changes in tribal religion.
"Destroy the cultus of a village or nation too ruth-

lessly by missionary propaganda and you risk destroying the whole of its moral and social organisation." A few years ago I had the curious experience of being invited to attend (as an Anglican representative) a Roman Catholic Foreign Missionary Exhibition and Conference held in London. The cardinal presided, and the most interesting speech (to me at any rate) was one delivered by an earnest Jesuit in which he contrasted our Protestant missions in a certain diocese in Africa with the work done by his own communion, and claimed that we were giving the people stones for bread, because we were unsympathetic to their native customs and love of ceremonial. Non-Roman missions however (whether Anglican or otherwise) will probably dispute the necessity for what they feel to be a pandering to the unregenerate instincts of primitive pagans, and will point to their own admittedly large rolls of earnest church-members; while it will not be forgotten that the African clergy of a certain evangelical diocese not long ago refused to unite in provincial organisations with their neighbouring Anglo-Catholic brethren, and replied (with a quaint reminiscence of the good and wild olive of Romans xi): "No, they are the wild bananas and we are the good bananas."

Has not in fact the vast experiment of Latin and eastern orthodox Christianity made too great a surrender? Our view of the universe and especially our knowledge of the history of the earth has changed so surprisingly during the last two generations that instead of thinking of the age-long tradition of the

Church as something fixed from which we are bound
to proceed, we are invited to regard the great conception of God unfolded in Jesus of Nazareth as
still relatively new. "Christianity," we are told, "is
a very young religion," and I submit that the greater
part of its expression for the past eighteen hundred
years at any rate has been of the nature of an
experiment, based on the assumption that a complete breach with natural religion was unnecessary.

The net result of the Protestant Reformation
350 years ago was to initiate a break with that
experiment. Thoroughgoing Protestants have made
a complete breach with the past, or have at any
rate tried to do so. Anglicans and some others have
felt that a middle course was the wiser one. They
have let themselves be guided by the feeling that
a sober moderation dictated by respect for varying
temperaments was better than a one-sided radicalism,
and so they have produced a scheme which the
experience of our generation seems to be justifying
in an unexpected way, and in which people of
Catholic and Protestant temperaments are invited
to try to live and worship together and respect one
another. It is hard to see how anyone can read
such a book as Prof. Pratt's work on *The Religious
Consciousness* without feeling how necessary some
such scheme is, and how unfruitful a merely partisan
organisation of religion is bound to prove. But
whether we be Anglicans or no, the spirit of the
past Reformation pledges us in loyalty to remain
free to develop in harmony with whatever new
knowledge may come to us, to keep clear of beggarly

rudiments and to be no more entangled again in a yoke of bondage.

If we compile a census of the professing Christians who inhabit the earth, it is certainly alarming to note that the vast majority belong to some section or other of the great bodies which have worked along the lines of the older syncretism. Protestantism is still numerically a limited element except on its American side, where it is probably the most potent missionary force in the world.

But to be unduly influenced by such considerations is to make a grave mistake. There is nothing either in the doctrines of science or the dictates of reason which proclaims that the truth of a certain belief is to be measured by the number of persons by whom at any given moment it is held. A true belief may be held by a handful of honest and intelligent people and denied or scoffed at by a vast mass of ill-educated, prejudiced, or misinformed persons. If it be true it may come to be universally held; but if mixed with error its universal acceptance may be hindered for many generations if not indefinitely postponed, because the exposure of the error may at any time tend to discredit the truth that goes with it. I am most anxious to avoid any appearance of injustice or prejudice. It is impossible to study Catholic Christianity without being impressed by its depth and richness. I can never forget the words of Baron von Hügel (7): "Protestantism ...so pathetically understandable, yet so largely unjust because ungenerous." I desire with all my heart to avoid any semblance of ungenerosity.

But I find it impossible to believe that the grand task of making essential Christianity the common world religion has passed entirely beyond the stage of experiment, and that the latter has been decided in one particular way. It seems to me that the experiment has been only partially successful because it has made much too unfavourable a treaty with the natural religious systems of mankind, and by unwarrantable surrenders to their less worthy features has seriously endangered its future. On the other hand, lest I fall into just that ungenerosity which I wish to avoid, let it be admitted that many of the past leaders of Latin Christianity have been strongly opposed to undue syncretism. Thus St Martin of Tours, St Boniface and others like them acted very sternly in destroying the insignia of heathenism, while in the English penitentials and canons as well as in the canons of sixth century continental councils may be found frequent denunciations of heathen usages. Gregory the Great himself stopped the cult of sacred trees at Terracina[8]. But I am not speaking of special instances so much as of the general trend and temper of ecclesiastical policy, and of this it seems impossible to form any other conclusion. If the leaders of the Church held any stricter views they were at any rate powerless or unwilling to prevent laxer ones from ultimately prevailing, and these in some of the most important features of cultus and devotion. It was perhaps the pious laity rather than the clergy who were responsible for these laxities, but the clergy at any rate have shown them culpable tolerance.

The surrender for instance to the widespread instinct of simple people to worship the female principle in nature and the attempt to satisfy it by the cultus of the Blessed Mother of Christ finds no real support in the documentary evidence of what Jesus of Nazareth really taught, and can only be justified by such a handling of texts as a scientific historian could not possibly tolerate. In the same way the cultus of the localised presence in the consecrated elements of the Communion Service (as sharply to be distinguished from a real and objective spiritual presence of our Lord in the midst of the faithful gathered together at that service to bless them and feed their souls with the strength of His own life-giving personality), this cultus is, I repeat, an obvious development along the lines of traditional natural religion. The cultus of consecrated food and drink occurs in connection with pagan sacramental meals, and is a feature in many religions alike in Greece, Mexico, Russia, Tartary and Peru[9]. Even Fr Delehaye[10] draws a comparison between the ordinary service of exposition of the Blessed Sacrament and the service of exposition of Nile water in a pyx by a priest of Isis as depicted upon a fresco preserved in the Naples Museum, just as he also does between the detrition of the statue of St Peter at Rome and that of Hercules at Agrigentum, in both cases by the kisses of the worshippers. He adds the following somewhat unconvincing defence: "The same thought, under analogous circumstances, has found expression after an interval of centuries in identical actions and attitudes. Concerning this

point it appears to me that no further discussion
is called for." The practice of reservation of the
sacramental elements for purposes of adoration, and
the service of benediction are so plainly an accommodation to the feelings of those who have expressed
their devotion in some form of idolatry that it is
difficult to see any flaw in the logic of the Jesuit
missionary Ricci who petitioned the Pope to tolerate
the expression by Chinese Christians of respect for
their ancestors by allowing them to burn incense in
front of their ancestral tablets. It must be granted
that many ceremonial practices may be justified
on the lines of the philosophy of " as if." For example
M. Le Roy (11) says that in the case of verbal symbols
such as, "God is our Father," we are to behave to
God *as if* He were our Father, without for a moment
supposing that the verbal symbol exhausts the
whole conception of what God stands for: and he
goes on to say that in the presence of the consecrated Host in the monstrance or tabernacle we
ought to have the same feeling *as if* we were in
the presence of the visible Jesus. The two little
words which are emphasised plainly expose the
whole structure of this system of devotion. They
can be used to justify all the extravagances of relic-
worship, and the veneration of images. It is doubtful
however whether those who profess this philosophy
are quite aware of the curious ways in which it may
be and is employed. For example, in the directions
for Buddhist devotion the worshipper is enjoined to
offer flowers or incense before the image of the
Buddha just *as if* the Buddha were present and

able to derive pleasure from the offering, when of
course it is known all the time that according to
the actual teaching of Buddhism the Buddha has
long since been absorbed into the ocean of Nirvana
and is no longer in existence, so that he cannot
possibly be conscious of the devotion which is being
offered to him (12). The only effect that can possibly
ensue must be an effect on the character of the
worshipper. Now this kind of doctrine is plainly a
wolf in sheep's clothing. It is only rationalism
masquerading in the guise of simple faith. The
honesty of the new learning will always revolt
against what must seem to it a system of pious
fraud: either a thing is true or it is not true.

This however does not get over the difficulty that
acting upon a certain doctrine as though it were
true produces certain results. The point is that the
results are produced by the honesty of the devotion.
If therefore the object of devotion is discredited, the
remedy for this disaster is not to give up worshipping
altogether but to find something else which is true
and worship that, and therefore the main duty of
the prophets of any religion at any given time must
be to provide for the public the most complete
truth about God that is possible at that time, and
not to bolster up the expression of religious devotion
by the introduction or maintenance of devotional
practices which are not based on the actual truth
so far as it is known but which simply appeal to
some element in the subconscious lumber-room
where mankind has chosen to stow the cast-off
clothing of its earlier beliefs.

I shall probably be told that I have made the elementary mistake of not allowing enough for the non-rational element in religion, and for the instincts of primitive peoples and of women of limited intelligence. I shall be reminded that the sense of awe and reverence ought to be maintained, and that this can be done more successfully by continuing the use of pious ceremonies which keep alive the deepest elemental instincts of mankind, than by a bare and gaunt policy of iconoclasm. I can only reply to this that I have not underrated the importance of such matters. It is obvious that some people are sacramentalists and others are not. Let us take for an example the cultus of the Black Virgin of Chartres. Here we have an extremely popular and ancient devotion which is not difficult to defend. I sat and watched it for about an hour not many months ago. The image in question is not of the Virgin alone, but of the Virgin and Holy Child. The colouring is meant to remind the worshipper that the originals were Syrians, and therefore "dark whites." We need not trouble ourselves with the tales current about its origin. Suffice it to say that day by day, and year by year, there is to be seen an unceasing stream of devout persons who come and kneel in the presence of this small statuette, burn their votive candles, say prayers, and reverently kiss the pillar on which it stands. The swarthy figures are a vivid reminder to these worshippers of the origin of their religion, and it may be argued that for peasants and non-intellectuals the simple devotion is harmless and affectionate. It is all very un-English, no doubt, and our friends from the East will tell us that they can parallel the externals quite easily from popular Hinduism or Mahayana Buddhism; indeed it is not quite certain whether the difference is not to some extent one of fashion rather than principle. The cultus of the Nightingale and Cavell statues, and of the cenotaph with its masses of flowers, to say nothing of local war-shrines—all this is an indication that even the undemonstrative Englishman has his own way of doing these things.

"Idolatry is an aid to worship which is quite innocent and natural in some peoples, but which the Jews never understood." (13) Will it surprise some to know that that remark comes from the writings of the present Dean of St Paul's, a Protestant mystic if ever there was one, and no advocate of any traditional cultus? I should not wish to overemphasise what the Dean might say after all is a mere *obiter dictum*, but the fact remains that the performance of certain manual acts in the presence of symbolical objects still induces devotional feelings, and stimulates the religious consciousness in a way which many think to be highly beneficial. The traditionalist will say, "Let such acts go on, even if we know that they are in no way necessary to the honour and glory of God, even if they have a bad history behind them. They are the language of the heart rather than of the intellect, and should not be discouraged....Idolatry in the sense of the use of symbols as an aid to concentration at a certain stage of religious development is both useful and harmless. The second commandment is no more literally binding upon Christians than the fourth. The one needs interpretation as much as the other. It is kept only in the literal sense by the Moslems, and the cinematograph and other agencies, such as the illustrated paper, are now breaking down their rigidity in this respect. The whole problem of the heathen in his blindness who bows down to wood and stone needs re-consideration." The answer to such an *apologia* must necessarily depend on a large number of factors, including the temperament and educational level of the worshippers, the nature of the dogma implied by the ceremonial, and the experience of the effect in all religions of an accumulation of such ceremonial. But there can be little doubt that a close adherence to the prophetic teaching of Jesus must always have the effect of severely pruning and limiting ceremonial and of curtailing or more correctly of sublimating the primitive instinct which associates religious devotion chiefly with external acts and with the use of concrete images.

I have spoken so far almost entirely of traditional religious practices in what may be called Catholic Christianity. It is curious however to note that especially in this country and in the United States of America Reformed Christianity has found itself either unable or unwilling to discard one definite element of traditional supernaturalism. I mean, of course, the superstitious reverence for the text of the Bible. The cultus of sacred books and papers, and indeed of writings of any kind, is something which comes down to man from his remote past, and he is so tenacious of it that even within the last hundred years, in spite of the assaults of critical study, the continent of America has presented us with two perfectly new sacred books, while on both sides of the Atlantic many of the most earnest Christians still adhere with stubborn tenacity to the infallibility of the old Scriptures. No further back than 1913 a large and important missionary body in Africa was circulating in one of its native churches a summary of the Old Testament with Abp. Ussher's chronology printed at the top of each page, while a large number (I had almost said all that I have seen) of Elementary Catechisms which are published for use in African missions still teach the literal truth of the story of Adam and Eve. Recent controversies have shown that the pragmatic effects (both in the mission field and at home) of implicit faith in the verbal inspiration of the Bible are far from spent, and it must be confessed that the beneficial nature of such effects may be used to justify the belief quite as reasonably as the beneficial effects of the cultus of the reserved Sacrament may be used to justify a certain sort of eucharistic doctrine.

There is a strange use of the Bible which is called mystical and which depends largely upon patristic practice. I quote from a recent sermon preached in Oxford cathedral (14). "There is," says the preacher, "a distinction which we must often remember as we read the Old Testament. It is the distinction between the original meaning of the words and the meaning which they now have for us. In early days the Jews were accustomed to treat their literature very freely. They combined old materials in a new way; they corrected and added to what they found; and as their interest in religion deepened, they put new and higher meanings upon old and familiar words. When the Christian Church took over the Old Testament from the Jews, it used a similar freedom. It did not, indeed, further alter the words which it found; we read them to-day much as our Lord must have read them. But the fuller knowledge which the Church possessed enabled her teachers to find in the Old Testament a deeper meaning than even the Jews had found; and it is with this deeper meaning that we are chiefly concerned to-day. What the words originally meant often matters little; what they mean as part of the Bible matters a great deal. The Bible is the Church's book; we interpret it rightly when we interpret it in accordance with the Church's mind." According to this the whole of the Psalter may and should still be used in public worship, because of the interpretation which the Church puts upon it. But I ask five questions here. What does the preacher mean by "The Church" in this instance? Does he mean the Church of the 39 Articles, or the Latin Church in the days of St Ambrose, or the Church of the Palestinian Jewish Christians, or the Church in Russia before the Revolution? By the practice of what Church can we Christians possibly be bound to-day? Is it possible to handle the Old Testament any longer with honesty and profit in the way in which pre-critical persons handled it? And, has the preacher any conception of the way in which the plain layman regards such subtleties, and does he wish to keep that layman in the Church? It is true of course that a certain method of biblical exegesis was accustomed to see types and shadows of the New Testament everywhere in the Old. It is even arguable that our Lord during His earthly ministry accommodated Himself to the customs of His contemporaries in His use of the text of the Old Testament, and that His apostles followed suit. But unless we disbelieve in the guidance of the living Spirit of Jesus, and hold ourselves literally bound by His earthly actions during the days of His flesh, we cannot rest content with such exegesis to-day. The idea that the words of a psalm can mean anything that the Church likes them to mean is really, if we face its implications, a superstitious idea. It revolts our British sense of honesty and straightforwardness. I know of course that its advocates are quite sincere, and that their piety, eloquence and earnestness render the idea less repulsive than it might seem if less attractively presented. But they are hopelessly out of touch with the real world, and if they seek to evangelise that real world by making assent to this fantastic use of documents part of their gospel, the real world will not for long listen to them. Even the revised lectionary of the Church of England still reveals a good deal of that mystical use of the Old Testament which is repugnant to the plain layman, and suggests that when its compilers drew it up the veil was still to a great extent over their

faces, even as it lay on the faces of many Jews of
Paul's day when Moses was read to them. This
attitude towards the text of the Bible, prominent
as it is among the Protestant bodies, is not confined
to them. In the year 1920 Pope Benedict XV issued
the Encyclical "Spiritus Paracletus" in which he
taught that although many things are said in
Scripture which seem incredible, nevertheless they
are true; that the very notion of error in its ut-
terances is inadmissible; that Scripture may seem
to contradict itself, but in reality it does not; and
that to doubt the freedom of Scripture from error
is impious. What more could any bibliolater desire?
What essential difference is there between this and
the Moslem notion of the infallibility of the Koran?
Such a doctrine of inspiration degrades the Christians
who hold it to the level of the heathen around them.

I submit that the time has come when the Spirit
of Christ is calling the Churches throughout the
world to consider whether the experiment of a one-
sided treaty with traditionalism has proved an un-
qualified success. "He that hath an ear, let him
hear what the Spirit saith unto the churches."

The general situation is one of great interest. Out
of a world-population of 1646 millions the Roman
communion comprises still the larger part of the 564
millions of Christians—(that is if we take the figures
of 1920)—so that for many enquirers it appears as
the normal expression of Christianity in the world
to-day. It retains its more or less invincible position
by its strong discipline, by its massive witness to
the supernatural, which is attractive to many outside

its ranks, and by the policy of accommodation to
natural religion which it has long pursued. It is rich
in saints, and its position has enabled it in the past
to bring under its yoke a large amount of the art
and literature and ethical enthusiasm of mankind.
It shows admirable judgment in handling souls, and
a knowledge of the psychology of religion in all its
essentials though under a different name. Not a few
members of an influential group in the Church of
England to-day are desirous of bringing English
Christians more closely into relation to this great
communion; and to some extent a good case can be
made out for their policy. Anglo-Saxon Christianity
certainly is in many important matters defective. It
is provincial and insular; it is often disfigured by
banality and irreverence; it shows comparatively
little discipline and *esprit de corps*; it has frequently
been clumsy and stupid in the use it has made of
the many beautiful buildings which it has inherited.
Worse still, it has been contemptuous of asceticism
and has been inclined to discount or explain away
the hard sayings and heroic appeals which are to be
found in the gospels. Sober worldliness has been its
dominant note. To all who feel the appeal of
romanticism, and the glories of mediaeval religion
when at its best, the attraction of Catholicism must
always be magnetic. Having felt it myself and
having in undergraduate days experienced under its
spell something which I can only describe as conversion, I venture to think that I can speak with
sympathy in this matter.

But there are difficulties, serious difficulties on

the other side. The great fault about Rome as we
see it at present is not that it wants to be Catholic
in spirit but that in spite of all its successful propaganda it has so far only succeeded in being
Mediterranean in expression. And yet a reformed
Rome (if such were possible) and a Catholicism freed
from obscurantist tendencies would attract very
many of us. To be *semper eadem* is all very well if it
is a matter of loyalty to the Spirit of Jesus, but not if
it is chiefly a matter of rite, cultus, and philosophy;
and in any case adherence to bad history and false
criticism of the documents of Christianity does not
argue well for the future. It can hardly be to the
advantage of an enlightened Christianity that the observance of the anniversary of a legendary Assumption should be so zealously advocated. Churches
which, whether they be continental or insular, desire
to be Catholic in the sense of embracing large masses
of the population, also tend inevitably to whittle
down their ethical standard to the level of the man
in the street in order to retain him as a member,
with the net result that Christian morals in such
cases gradually come in the end to mean almost
nothing at all. They seem to the outside observer
to advocate a mere system of insurance against the
future rather than a falling in love with God and
man. Moreover nobody can deny that there is a
very considerable shrinkage on the part of the
traditionalist Churches all over the world, a shrinkage
which is not due to the moral turpitude of mankind,
but to the wholly innocent tendency of the younger
minds everywhere to look forward rather than back

for truth, and to drop quietly everything which does not seem honestly to fit in with the features of the real world as they experience it. The whole basis of institutional Christianity seems to them to consist in an appeal to the past. Expressions such as—the faith of the ages, the primitive Church—the Church has always taught—from the earliest times there have been—and so forth and so on, which are widely current among the official teachers of Christianity, conflict seriously with the mode of thought and instruction which has been popularised during the last fifty years. The appeal to the authority of the past has been still further weakened by the European disaster of 1914 and succeeding years, and by the apparent ineffectiveness of organised religion in trying to avert that disaster.

The popularisation of the empirical study of the sciences has brought an increasing number of persons in touch with what the religiously-minded feel to be a vast new revelation of the ways of God in nature, a revelation which has dwarfed the significance of pre-scientific religious beliefs. Modern education proceeds on the lines of the aphorism, that to distrust one's father and mother is the first commandment with promise. Reasonable proofs of the truth of everything taught are expected to be given, and if they are not given there is immediate dissatisfaction. The full effect of this has not yet had time to show itself, but it must be plain that it will before long profoundly affect all those Church systems which were framed at a time when it was supposed that only a minority of persons would ever be in a position to read and write, and when the idea of natural law was almost unknown.

The essential point however which I wish to affirm in this lecture is that traditionalism as we have surveyed it is not only a method by which in the past men have sought to embody the Spirit of Christ, but that it is to-day in a particular aspect a very serious rival to vital Christianity especially in this country, and a positive hindrance to the spiritual progress of mankind. It badly wants to be the religion of to-day, regardless of the question of whether it is likely to be the religion of to-morrow. Timid souls who fear the loss of the religious values they have come to prize are apt to regard it as the sole breast-work against an advancing tide of unbelief. One must admit that its accumulated experience of the past cannot be dismissed with a wave of the hand, and is impressive, if not convincing at every point. But that experience is more fruitful in its knowledge of human nature than in its knowledge of God. It is an easier and shorter business to know man than to know God, and an astute ecclesiasticism that is able successfully to manage men and appeal to their feelings does not take nearly so long to acquire as a knowledge of God, which is much more hardly won and does not carry with it nearly so popular an appeal. I hope that the religious leaders of this country at any rate will not be misled into making terms with ecclesiastical traditionalism. It is true that its rejection may mean the loss to organised religion of a number of persons who are really attracted by signs and wonders and who prefer a cloudy superstition to clear faith. These people, like the Raskolniks of Russia will perhaps take refuge in a kind of non-juring Church of their own. Fundamentalism in America has behind it, no doubt, the support of many persons of wealth and influence, and enjoys the service of many devoutly religious enthusiasts who blindly suppose that they are serving the cause of Jesus Christ in rejecting the claims of honest scholarship, and it may succeed for a time in a most effective persecution of the modernists; but it is impossible for it to maintain itself indefinitely in the face of plain facts. Traditionalism gains its adherents by its appeal to a number of elemental passions and prejudices of the human spirit, but it yields to them far more than Jesus of Nazareth was ever willing to yield, and that is why it is possible for a dis-tinguished Roman-Catholic layman to say that all religious *institutions* without exception are at their worst in the matter of their relations with science and scholarship (15).

Does it seem unnecessary to point out the im-possibility of reconciling the teaching of Jesus Christ with the peculiar though perfectly sincere methods which have been adopted in the endeavour to place all manner of traditional cults at least nominally under His protection, and to provide a place for Him in the natural religions of mankind without disturbing them too much? Is it not possible that they are right who declare that we do actually need what has been called a fresh reformation, in which the resources of history, science and psycho-

logy are enlisted in constructing a new and better
plan for making the Kingdom of Christ effective on
this planet? Reformations however are not begun
by clergy sitting round a table and passing resolutions. Like religions, they grow spontaneously, and
those who come after us may be able to look back
and say that long before the date of these lectures
a new Reformation had already started. It is not
good to be self-conscious. Let us turn away from
ourselves and contemplate for a few moments the
principles of Jesus Christ.

He never preached the destruction of the religious
system which He found, but declared that He came
to fulfil and enrich it. He praised the steward who
brought out of his treasure things new and old. His
followers represent Him as promising that His spirit
shall dwell with them always, not only to interpret
the past but to lead into new truth. In the face of
these facts it is hard to suppose that the Church of
the future can possibly be the exact facsimile of any
single one of the various Christian organisations and
denominations which exist to-day, though it is safe
to believe that whatever treasures they possess will
find a place in it, with the addition of many things
that remain even yet unknown.

Jesus Christ set a little child as the model for His
disciples. It has unfortunately been assumed that
this meant that He praised unquestioning faith and
absence of intellectual enquiry. There is no real
evidence that this is the case. Children, to begin
with, are not in the habit of taking things as they
find them. They are for ever asking questions, and

approach the world with fresh minds, and so they often see the truth which escapes the complexity of the adult intelligence. Christ never taught men to be childish or to love foolish immaturity in preference to growth in wisdom, but against the jaded prejudices of the traditionalists He set the freshness of the sincere and open mind, unspoilt and vigorous. The "wise and prudent" of his day were not independent thinkers, but hidebound commentators. The child trusts, it is true, but only because it is dealt with fairly. A child unfairly treated soon learns by bitter experience to be suspicious. Christ taught that men might trust God because God could always be depended upon to treat them fairly. The heavenly Father as presented by Christ never tricks mankind by pretending that life is easy when it is not, but says: "Life is no easier for me than it is for you. I am only asking you to share my life. Knowing as you do that I love you, you can trust me, and I will lead you along the path of adventure and in the end to victory."

Christ never Himself approved of the use of miracles as a test of His authority. A wiser and humbler survey of all the evidence has led men to-day to believe that He did possess exceptional powers over nature and over the human body, but we directly disobey His plain commands if we isolate the use of such powers as evidence and try to impress untrained minds by using it as proof of His divine authority. "An evil generation seeketh after a sign," He said, and again, almost bitterly, "Except ye see signs and wonders ye will not believe." Supernaturalistic dualism may be a convenient bridge from this world into the world of spirit, but I for one can never believe either that it is a necessary bridge or that Christ wished us to make use of it.

Christ seems to have thought and spoken of God in terms familiar to some of the Hebrew prophets as shepherd, and of mankind as His flock. But the metaphor is easily misunderstood. The sheep of Christ's teaching are not blindly driven but intelligently led. It is curious that anyone can recite Ps. xxiii without noticing this, and it is well nigh heart-breaking to think that nearly the whole of western pastoral theology seems to have been constructed from the idea that there is a broad highway paved with the deposit of faith along which it is the duty of the minister to drive his flock, instead of which Christ pictures him as leading them on an expedition.

Christ, in spite of the fact that He Himself made no open protest against the actual worship of the temple at Jerusalem, and left a large liberty to His followers in their employment of the arts in the service of religious fellowship, set little store by the current devotions of natural religion. It is an uncomfortable fact that He seems to have definitely disapproved of the sort of vain repetitions which have been perpetuated in the use of the rosary, and it is not quite certain that He would have liked our litanies.

Jesus Christ did not teach men to regard religion as a system of insurance based upon rewards and punishments, with self-preservation and self-interest as the dominant motives. Religion to Him meant falling in love with God and one's neighbour, and while He emphasises, it is true, the ideal of moral justice and a sharp antithesis between good and evil He tells men that if they start out to seek salvation for themselves they will not find it: they must forget themselves. This is not traditionalist religion, which generally tends to be a business transaction, in which God is used for our benefit and safety.

During the past half century two main attempts have been made to account for Christianity as we see it to-day. On the one hand there is the kernel and the husk theory, commonly associated with Harnack. On the other is the acorn and the oak theory set forth by Loisy. The explanation favoured in this lecture will not fall into either class. I do not suppose for a moment that the whole of absolute religious truth can be limited to a single dogma as the kernel, nor do I agree on the other hand that the largest and most popular existing body of Christians is necessarily the one which best interprets the mind of Christ. What I am suggesting here is that in the career of Christ a particular group of ideas was given to religion, and that all the resources of the various nations of the world have something to contribute to the interpretation of that group of ideas, but that the function of the Christian group or complex is normative rather than in itself final, and that we can no more look to Galilee than to Rome for such finality. I firmly believe however that the normative group of ideas which was given

to us by Christ is certainly meant to serve as a check
and test of development. Call it, if you like, a complex *abc*. There may be added to it from other
sources in the process of time other elements *defg*
and so on to infinity. But these new elements, while
complementing the original complex *abc*, must never
be opposed to it, as they certainly will be in the
case of an unwise syncretism.

It is strange to reflect that the chief objection to
Christianity which had to be met by the early
apologists was that it was too new and young a
religion, and had behind it no respectable record of
antiquity. The apologists acted rightly in glorifying
the pure morals and simple faith of the Church as
contrasted with the puerile and often disgusting
mythologies of heathenism. But they made a fatal
mistake when they took a leaf out of the book of
the heathen and sought to show that they had a
longer pedigree by trying to prove the prior antiquity
of Moses. I often wish they had said boldly, "Yes,
ours *is* a new faith, and a plague on your antiquity!"
Yet many apologists to-day follow their lead and
talk much about the "faith of the ages" and the
peril of being modern.

The Christian religion as presented in certain
quarters, and as unfortunately a great many people
expect to hear it expounded, is a dull traditionalism.
It has been shorn of its radiance. It has become a
study of pundits, a solace for the middle-aged, a
hobby for the retired, a cult for pensioners in com-
fortable watering-places and health-resorts. Youth
passes it by. Yet the truth all the time is that the

doctrine of the likeness of God set forth by Jesus Christ is ever new and ever modern. Just as the quantum theory is regarded by some as the first real law of nature to be discovered, because it is quite unlike what we should have invented for our-selves, so the doctrine of God set forth in Jesus Christ is unlike that which the natural instincts of mankind would have invented. It conflicts with natural religion. It conflicts with much of our limited human experience. The omnipotence of love and the inclusion of the Deity within the sphere of suffering and struggle are a paradox and an offence which may well for that reason be true. This doctrine of God is not something which we inherit, but which makes no demands on our conduct and behaviour. It has to be new in each one of us. We are not born Christians, we are born much more land-animals, and even the most exalted of us needs a new birth. In most of us there is, as long as we live, an unceasing conflict between our lower impulses and the ideal of Christ, and since the world is made up of such individuals the challenge of Christ to the world is always being made afresh. It is quite fair to retort when some would appeal to the primitive Church as a thing of the past: "*We* are the primitive Church."

For indeed the Christian religion compared with the age of the earth is a new and infant creation. The eyes of its founder as He hung on the Cross were fixed upon a future which is still immeasur-ably far ahead of us. We are only just beginning to emerge from one temporary aspect of the universe into another, and the whole of the past expression of the Christian spirit has been as much limited and conditioned by that older view as any other part of the inheritance of mankind. But there is no sign that the Kingdom of God as inaugurated by Christ has yet completed its establishment, and become a back-number. On the contrary, we observe a steady and inward reconstruction of religion, a perishing of old forms in order that new and better ones may take their place; and in this process we see thoughtful Christians playing their part, feeling no disloyalty to their Master in doing so, since they recognise that it is just loyalty to Him which demands their share in progressive religious movements, so long as they observe His general principle that it is better to fulfil than to destroy.

The disciples of Christ have tried making experiments in the direction of a treaty with various types of traditionalism, and in the process they have learned many lessons, but if the shrinkage of their influence which we see to-day really means, as I believe it does, a relaxation of grip for the purpose of securing a tighter hold, that fresh hold will only be secured by an absolute and impartial devotion to truth, whether it be the truth in the lessons already learnt, or the truth into which the Holy Spirit may choose to lead us in the future. It will not be secured by any endeavour, however well-intentioned, to place a particular party or school of thought in a position of intellectual supremacy, since in the now-familiar words of Archbishop Temple: "If the conclusions are prescribed the study is precluded."

RELATIVISM

CHRISTIANITY FINAL—IN WHAT SENSE?

WE have before us to-day a perfectly clear issue. It may best be summed up in the question attributed to John the Baptist: "Art thou He that should come, or do we look for another?" If it be granted that religion is able to make good its claim against secularism, if it be granted that Christian theism is preferable to any species of pantheism, if it be granted further that the experiment of making a treaty with traditional religion in order to graft Christian theism on to it has proved rather wasteful —it still remains a question whether in Christian theism we possess a doctrine of God which is unsurpassable.

Various causes contribute to the raising of this question. There is, to begin with, the idea that evolutionary progress is applicable to religion. Many persons suppose that because primitive man seems to possess a rudimentary religion, therefore our religion to-day stands in a kind of middle position, while the young woman whom Mr Shaw represents as being hatched out of an egg in the year 31,920 A.D. will have a much more perfect religion than ours; and this supposition is by no means an entirely foolish one. In the second place, travel and study have made us all so much better acquainted with one another's beliefs that we are finding it an increasingly distasteful matter to criticise them. This has led, in the third place, to a kind of application of the theory of relativity to religion. We may almost say in fact that in the opinion of some persons the Christian who lives in the heart of a Christian community is inside one frame of reference, and the Moslem who inhabits Arabia is in another frame of reference, while the Confucian and the Buddhist are yet again in other separate frames. This point of view has been expressed in a very extreme form by the late Prof. Ernst Troeltsch(1). "Christianity," he says, "could not be the religion of such a highly developed racial group if it did not possess a mighty spiritual power and truth; in short, if it were not, in some degree, a manifestation of the Divine Life itself. The evidence we have for this remains essentially the same, whatever may be our theory concerning absolute validity—it is the evidence of a profound inner experience. This experience is undoubtedly the criterion of its validity, but, be it noted, only of its validity *for us*. It is God's countenance as revealed to us; it is the way in which, being what we are, we receive and react to the revelation of God. It is binding upon us, and it brings us deliverance. It is final and unconditional for us, because we have nothing else, and because in what we have we can recognise the accents of the Divine voice. But this does not preclude the possibility that other racial groups, living under entirely different cultural conditions, may experience their contact with the Divine Life in quite a different way, and may themselves also possess a religion which has grown up with them, and from which they cannot sever themselves so long as they remain what they are. And they may quite sincerely regard this as absolutely valid for them, and give expression to this absolute validity according to the demands of their own religious feeling." Dr Troeltsch indeed has developed a theory of what he calls polymorphous truth, i.e. that truth is utterly different for different times and races.

The question has therefore come to be asked—"Is there any sense in which the Christian religion can be regarded as final? Is there any element in it which can be regarded as in a scientific sense possessing absolute validity?" If Christianity has a relative validity in comparison with all other existing religious systems, in what sense, if in any, may we believe it to be the final word in religious truth?

There are here in fact two distinct problems which arise out of the twofold claim which the Christian religion has always made. It has always claimed to supersede all other existing systems. The Figure standing at its centre has ever since the age of the New Testament documents been believed to be the Lord of the world, not of any one continent, and this assumption underlies the whole fabric of Christian missionary effort. It is only recently that we have been able to get a reasonable account of the other two great missionary movements of this planet, Moslem and Buddhist, and interesting as they prove to be, the Christian story still remains the most remarkable and most impressive of the three.

But more than this; the figure standing at the centre of the Christian religion is believed to be the individual embodiment of a certain absolute and final religious truth, beyond which in its knowledge of God and of the art of right living the human race is not going to advance.

Now it must be noted that these claims are neither academic nor new. They come before us supported by an immense mass of solid experience. It is not a question of counting heads, but of recognising the way in which all over the planet the figure of Christ has tended to supplant other figures as the object of religious devotion. Even the cultus of the Mother of Christ cannot really drive out the devotion to Him which expresses itself in various forms of sacramental cultus. A series of maps will very soon show how universally it has been possible to plant the Christian system of life. The number of disciples in any given locality may not be large, but the character of those disciples is recognisable, and establishes the claim that the Christian religion is able to build its distinctive and peculiar type of character in any quarter of the globe, while the Moslem and Buddhist movements seem to be hampered wherever the climate is cold. It is also fairly obvious that the success of Islam depends upon a relatively low moral appeal, while that of Buddhism depends upon the personality of its founder as an object of devotion rather than upon the pessimistic philosophy which he taught, and it cannot be denied that the tendency has been artificially to render that personality more attractive by the transference to it of features which are really the property of Jesus Christ.

The second claim comes before us supported by a similar body of testimony. Men and women repeatedly declare that in spite of the fact that for millions of persons who are acquainted with nothing better the religious systems of their own countries to a great extent satisfy their needs, yet those who have once become acquainted with what Christ has to offer them never show any desire to revert to their former systems because it is better. If they revert it is because the claims of Christ are too high for them, or because the pressure of social custom forces them back again into the old groove. Many for the same reason are secret disciples, who, though dissatisfied with their old religion, dare not openly declare their allegiance to the new. If the choice be that between one religion and another and not between religion and secularism, Christianity easily finds the first place, and it is noticeable that the modern pantheist almost invariably tries to give a Christian turn to his doctrines in order, as he thinks, to render them more attractive.

It is necessary however to enquire whether a modern scientific survey is able to confirm all this experience, and whether such a survey affords us any fresh and independent reasons for believing first that the Christian religion represents the highest known form of theism, and second that it contains the highest form of theism that can be known, and is therefore unsurpassable and final; and it is proper to enquire further in the third place in what respect

this so-called Christian theism is final and unsurpassable, since whatever permanent element it may
contain it must be plain to all that the Christian
complex contains both developments and accretions,
and many interesting and even useful accessories
whose value can only be temporary. We begin, then,
with the consideration of the first problem, that
created by the comparative study of religions. It
is commonly supposed that this branch of enquiry
has led to two consequences: (1) the accumulation
of a vast mass of conflicting values and types, from
which it is impossible to draw any safe conclusions,
(2) the obliteration for ever of the distinction between
natural and revealed religion. The distinction between
natural and revealed religion was in one sense a fair
attempt to account for experience. It is no doubt
true to say that all religions involve revelation as
well as discovery, and that on these lines it is impossible to set up a barrier between one and the
rest. But "barrier" is not the right word, because
it suggests an obstacle artificially erected, whereas
the distinction between Christianity and other religions is there to begin with, and invites explanation, and even if we say with Wendland that this
is a relative which afterwards merges into an absolute
distinction that is only a more scientific way of
saying what our forefathers were wont to put in
blunter language. With regard to the first consequence, we may say that it only follows when a
certain method is pursued, and it is by no means
certain that that method is ultimately going to
prove the best. There is undoubtedly a fine im-

partiality about the pages of the *Golden Bough*, and it would ill become me to depreciate in any way the noble and accurate industry of its author. But there are limits to what this kind of method will yield by way of results. It will tell us a great deal about the workings of the human mind face to face with the same natural phenomena at widely distant points on the earth's surface, and it will show us in what a vast number of different ways the human spirit is capable of describing such world-wide facts as birth, dreams, springtime, harvest, and sunset. But I do not think that the net result of all this vast enquiry, in which the anthropologists have played a most honourable part, has ever been more clearly summed up than in the words of Troeltsch in the third section of his famous little essay on the absolute validity of Christianity (2):

> This history of religion does not by any means provide us with a boundless mass of conflicting values. Quite the contrary. On investigation it shows remarkably few of such values, and very seldom discloses any spiritual goals which are actually new. Variety almost confines itself to the lower stages of religion, and there it is chiefly a variety of outward expression and ceremonial, slightly ruffling the surface of a great sea of monotony. The great creative powers of the inner life only begin to emerge in the higher stages, and the irruptions of such powers are not at all numerous. The seers who have had something new to tell humanity are rare, and it is astonishing on what a limited number of truths humanity has lived. In the comparative study of religion we are not faced with a wealth of religious forms about which we can never come to any decision, but only with a few great creations. The manifold religions of uncivilised peoples and their polytheisms have no significance in the quest after the highest religious values. There are but few great ethical and spiritual religions which build up a higher world in contradiction to the mere world of body and mind.

Troeltsch goes on to demonstrate that if the poly-theistic nature religions be left to themselves, there remain only two great groups which he describes perhaps in rather cumbersome fashion (though his meaning is quite clear) as (1) Prophetic-Christian-Platonic-Stoic religion; (2) Buddhistic-Oriental religion. Now I have ventured to devote my second lecture to an attempt to demonstrate the superiority of the first group to the second, but I am still faced with the two-fold task of showing for what reasons the Christian complex is believed to contain an element which is final and unsurpassable, and what that element is. It is to that therefore that we must now turn our attention.

Let us first of all go back and examine the causes which in the beginning opened the way for the Christian religion to assume a dominant position in the ancient world. Gibbon in his celebrated fifteenth chapter gives, it will be remembered, five reasons—the zeal of the primitive Church, the doctrine of the immortality of the soul, the possession of miraculous powers, the virtues of the first Christians, and the power of organisation shown in the government of the Church. Harnack (3), writing on the expansion of Christianity, says that it triumphed because it was a gospel of salvation and of love, a religion of spirit and of power shown in a new morality, a religion of authority and of reason, a religion which presented its adherents as the chosen people of God and could point to the fulfilment of prophecy. Loisy says that Christianity triumphed by syncretism. The late Dr Emmet (4) has summed the matter up a little differently. He is quite ready to grant that the success of organised Christianity on a large scale may well have been due to its treaty with the traditional faiths which it supplanted. But he goes on to point out, what even Loisy admits (5), that there were certain distinctive features in Christianity which counted most: that in spite of its willingness to treat with a certain amount of Pagan belief and practice, it still kept its own individuality, showed itself jealous of its own peculiar standing, and never entirely lost those features. He does not so completely despair of the human race as to hold that it accepted the Christian faith mainly upon irrational grounds, and he proceeds to enumerate what he considers to be the five distinctive features of primitive historical Christianity:

(1) An extraordinarily high, simple, and attractive doctrine of God.

(2) A totally new conception of man and his value to God.

(3) A clear statement of the relation of God to the material world.

(4) A redemption not merely of individuals (the Pagan mystery religions claimed to offer that) but of society as a whole. The world was to be saved by being transferred into the Kingdom of God.

(5) Christianity was as no other, the religion of hope.

I venture to develop a little Dr Emmet's fifth point. It seems to be of quite enormous importance that the Christian religion offers the human race a real reason for believing that the universe is not a fraud and a nightmare. The mere doctrine of

immortality as referred to by Gibbon does not strike
one as in itself a very good reason for the success
of Christianity. What men were longing to be told
was that the life after death in which they most of
them more or less believed was not a thing to be
dreaded. An immortality which was simply a con-
tinuation of the present very difficult life or a series
of monotonous cycles of re-birth did not offer much
attraction to the weary. An immortality which left
the poor struggling sinner, who had done his best,
to bear the consequences of his sins in his next re-
incarnation—this was something to be dreaded
indeed. But the Christian hope of the life of the
world to come offered men, as it still offers them,
comfort and courage by its firm assertion that for
the Christian believer who is sincere the future life
is one of progress to better things, and of a fellowship with one another in God. Similarly it is not
enough to say that Christianity offered men a very
high conception of God. That of course is true
enough. The Christian idea of a deity not merely
philanthropic but "philocosmic" (if I may coin a
word), of a self-sacrificing, loving Personal God,
stands by itself in history. But what men needed
and what they still need was and is some kind of
token that this benevolent and philocosmic God is
not engaged in a losing battle. Only the Christian
faith in the victorious Christ as a mighty living and
active Power in the lives of men has ever provided
such a token.

It will be seen that the reasons why the Christian
religion triumphed over its competitors in the period

of late antiquity are to a great extent the reasons which commend it to the world of to-day, and that they certainly operate in the mission field. The notion however that truth at any given point in the career of the human race is only partial and relative still lurks in the background and tends to unsettle men's minds. They think that because our knowledge of many of the mysteries of life has greatly increased since the foundation of Christianity, and especially during the last 120 years, it is therefore improbable that any kind of absolute truth can have been imparted to the human race so far back as 1900 years ago. They also feel, though with considerably less justification, that a religious doctrine which originated in one of the lesser Mediterranean provinces of the Roman Empire is likely to show a strongly-marked relative apprehension of truth rather than an absolute one. And further still, reckoning as they do the probability that the human race has still an immensely long career in front of it, they are tempted to speculate whether the future may not hold in store the rise of at least one if not more than one new religion. For these reasons, while men are disposed to regard the Christian religion as a phenomenon of great interest and nobility, and are prepared to study it with respect as one of the chief elements in the formation of the modern world, they are not confident of being able to put their whole trust in it. They are not sure enough of their ground to be able to accept the challenge of a popular preacher of to-day, and to stake everything from the clothes on their backs even to their existence itself upon its claim to finality. They are not prepared to bet their lives that Jesus Christ is the most perfect manifestation possible of the character of God.

Now I must own to a very great sympathy with this feeling of uncertainty, and I am sure that it is felt by many persons in direct proportion to the intensity of their religious earnestness. I want to try to do what I can not only to ease the discomfort which they feel but also to try to remove the uncertainty.

And first of all let me point out that while it is quite impossible to get any real knowledge of the alleged value of the Christian religion without making an act of faith in it which is equivalent to betting one's life on its truth, it is already possible to do the latter without prejudice to the future, because there is at least a strong inclination among religiously minded persons who are able to make an impartial survey of the facts in favour of the Christian doctrine of God and of human life, as being the best that we so far possess. That, at any rate, is something to go on with, and it enables many of us to say with Newman

> I do not ask to see
> The distant scene, one step enough for me.

Probability in the shape of reasonable inferences from data which in themselves do not furnish exhaustive proof is still the guide of life where natural science is concerned, and as far as probability goes, the balance still inclines upon the Christian side. The Christian complex is still the best general explanation of life. And next to this, the analogy of scientific experience leads us to the belief that though experience may deepen and widen, yet it never contradicts any genuine previous experience but only amplifies, fulfils and enriches it by fresh facts, and deductions therefrom. As Troeltsch declares: "Every truth which came to mankind at a later date would be bound to contain the truth enshrined in Christianity." (6)

But there is no need to stop here. There is a whole series of reasons for regarding the Christian declaration about God and life to be in certain senses both absolute and final.

Take it by itself first of all. It is its own best witness. The moment of its appearance in the world really does not matter, because, as I have pointed out before, what we may call the great creative period in religion is but a mere incident in the earth's history. The earliest creatures that might pass as human were in existence over 500,000 years ago, so that the entire career of humanity is only roughly a 2000th part of the age of the oldest rocks on the earth (7), while out of that 500,000 years only a little less than a 250th part can be allotted to the rise and progress of the Christian religion, and we have no records of any important religious creations which go back beyond (if indeed they go back as far as) the limit of the age of cultivation, 15,000 B.C. Although research may cause the figures which are offered us to vary slightly from time to time, the scale of calculation is so enormous that this statement may be left as it stands. The appearance of the great religions therefore is like a cluster of mountain peaks lying at the end of a great plain. The actual types of religion are not so much to be described as a chronological series, as a number of alternative solutions to the riddle of existence. Animism with its 10,000,000 daemons is one solution. Polytheism with its gods-many and lords-many is another. Pantheism is a definite solution. So is Deism. So also are Dualism and Atheism. These are all perennial answers to the perennial riddle. They are not orderly stages of development, but exist side by side on the planet, and the mind and heart of man try them in turn to see whether they can satisfy the restlessness which comes from having a life to lead and not knowing what to do with it. As against these the Christian complex is an alternative solution, and still stands in noble distinction from all the others. It has drawn its elements from varying sources, but I fail to see why the indebtedness of Jesus of Nazareth to His Jewish and Gentile background should in any way be held to diminish His unique greatness. We might just as well argue against the value of water because it can be split up into oxygen and hydrogen, or deny the aesthetic value of Wells cathedral by calling it a collection of stones. Jesus is the great personal centre round which all manner of human elements group themselves. There are however certain points in His solution of the problem of this planet which stand as an eternal antithesis to all others.

What are these points? They may be summed up as follows: The universe is the expression of the

thought of a Being who is no less than the highest
conception which we have of moral personality,
though He may well be much more. This Being may
be trusted: that is, I take it, the essence of what
Jesus means by calling Him Father. Instead of
being blind or capricious, He may be quite fairly
symbolised by the notion of wise and reasonable
parenthood. The universe being as great as it is
there are doubtless many different purposes being
worked out in it. But among these we can only
know that which concerns ourselves, nor need we
wish to know more, if God is to be trusted. But
further, Jesus proclaims this Being, whom He
symbolises as the Father, to be one whose aim, at
any rate as far as this planet is concerned, is to
produce an indeterminate number of individual
centres of consciousness and to give them the power
to win their freedom. So far as He chooses to control
these individuals He does so by impressing upon
them His intense desire to give Himself for them.
He wants His creatures to believe that He is the
essence of what they call love, and that He is no
remote being, but is actually within the circle of
the world's suffering and striving. The one thing
that matters in the eyes of this Deity is unselfish
service. It is plain that human beings will not be
content with the proclamation of such a god as
this. Such a god might be lovable and yet defeated
and destroyed by His own universe, which would
thus itself in the end prove to be the real god. Jesus
therefore goes on to show what He means us to take
as the forecast of the ultimate future. He submits

to crucifixion in order to put things to the test. The supreme test of God's love is that the spirit of God embodied in Jesus should be willing to suffer to the uttermost. The test of God's victory is that the living personality of Jesus and His message should not be crushed by the judicial murder of Calvary. The witness of history gives a conclusive answer on both these points. But the human soul asks one thing more. It asks that some assurance should be given it that the highest values it knows in human life, the values of personality and mutual love shall not be allowed to disappear in some infinite sea of undifferentiated being. Jesus affirms that the individual soul is of infinite worth to the being who has produced it, and in no single picture or parable does He merge the family of souls in the being of their parent, though He does make the permanence of the soul's blessedness depend upon its forgetfulness of self in this present state of existence, a forgetfulness which brings happiness and peace and the blessing of what is called "eternal life" here and now. Jesus also teaches us to discard the bargaining, cringing and servile type of prayer, so fatally common all over the world, in favour of a simple mystical harmonising of the human will with the divine. We are thus to cultivate an habitual state of trustful fearlessness.

It is idle to maintain that this view of the nature of God and the purpose of life is inseparably bound up with the ancient cosmogony and restricted view of the universe which the organised community of Christian believers has hitherto tended to associate with it. It is equally idle to deny that it has not made an immense difference to the relations between God and man and that therefore these relations have not been permanently changed by the career of Jesus. It also seems unreasonable to say that the Jesus of the gospels has not profoundly influenced the lives of countless millions who have lived since the days when He walked on earth. On the other hand I am quite ready to admit that we have not made the most of the wonderful things that Jesus of Nazareth has given us, and to believe that the impact of our changed views of the universe upon the Christian religion was necessary in order that the full and permanent value of the message of Jesus might be isolated and shine clearly. It is not presumptuous to say that we know more about the historical Jesus than, let us say, Athanasius or Leo, who after all were as far away from Bethlehem as we are from the days of the Tudors, and had far fewer devices open to them for establishing contact with historical personages who lived 300 to 400 years ago, than we have for establishing contact with personages of 2000 years ago. The permanent validity of the ethic of Jesus, challenged as it is by some, rests on just the very basis which might seem to invalidate it. It is an *Interimsethik*, in the sense that it does not deal with a developing society and provide detailed instructions for any one particular period, but with a state of society supposed to be on the eve of judgment in which only the big and fundamental things matter, so that all instructions deal purely with matters of principle, leaving details to be worked out as occasion arises. But if all men stand continually on the eve of judgment—*as they do*, then it is always the big things that matter, and so the proportions of the ethic of Jesus are permanently valid. What are we creatures of a day's probation compared with the eternal values of God? [8]

May one repeat that the moment of the appearance of Jesus does not diminish His authority over us because it occurred at a certain point in late antiquity? I know that Strauss declares that history is no place for absolute personalities. But it is a question whether Strauss was in a position to understand what he was talking about, since he was not a man of deep religious feelings. Still, of course, it is quite true that there is a real philosophical difficulty in the linking up of a religion which claims absolute validity and universality to an historical personality. Let us see what can be said about this difficulty.

First of all, are we so sure that the absolute does not reveal itself in a moment of history? Personal experience affirms that it does. It is often the case that the character of a human individual is revealed in his reaction to a single decisive event. Watch him at that time and you will know what he stands for in life. You may afterwards learn many other less important or even trivial things about him, but in that one decisive moment you will have come to know the one thing that matters about him, and although lesser instances of the same character may occur at many other times of his life, they will pass unnoticed, nor is it necessary that the decisive

moment should ever repeat itself. And again: there
is no individual alive, I believe, who cannot say that
somewhere in his or her life there was at least one
absolute and normative moment which did not repeat itself, and the memory and effect of which
determined the future development of that individual life. There may have been contact with
someone else, an interview with some great and
entrancing personality or some moment of intimate
friendship, the hearing of a sermon, the holding of
a conversation, the visiting of some famous spot,
or the experience of a great catastrophe. The "tolle
lege" of St Augustine is such an absolute moment.
The conversion of any person is such a moment. It
is a curious and undeniable fact of experience that
the Power behind the Universe does give the impression that at certain times it does take hold of
the course of one's life and shape one's ends in spite
of one's own inclinations. There is a curious "given-
ness" about some moments of life. (I speak of what
I know myself, of what perhaps all of us know.)
Life is not a dead level. It has its mountain peak
or peaks as well as its valleys and plains, and they
are encountered at no stated intervals or moments
during its course. Absolute moments in the history
of human development are certainly capable of
being discerned in other spheres than that of religion.
Why not also therefore in the sphere of religion
itself? Evolution, as has been pointed out, does not
account for every element in life. There are some
factors which are ends in themselves.

Consider here for a moment the amazing extent

to which for a brief period in the golden age of Athens, human thought got free, and how on a relatively low level of culture are to be found extraordinary flashes of very high artistic and philosophic inspiration. This brief period has never exactly repeated itself, but has remained absolute and normative for others which have followed it. It is admitted that the great thinkers of Greece are the intellectual parents of modern empirical science, and that they are still shaping the thought of the world to-day. The career and crucifixion of Jesus Christ are just such another absolute and normative group of events which continue to shape the thought of the world.

And next, let us remember that for a great mass of average humanity the concrete and historical is the natural way in which the abstract and universal is apprehended. Who will say that the Jesus of history does not still make a natural appeal to the fresh unprejudiced mind? I know that the objection is raised by a certain school of radical critics that Jesus of Nazareth is firmly rooted in His own age, and that it is only by modernising Him artificially that we can render Him attractive to the twentieth century; but the minister who possesses any pastoral experience knows that that objection is not true. Schweitzer himself is a witness against it. Think only of those memorable words which record, I suppose, his call to the Ogowe river: "He comes to us as one unknown, without a name, as of old by the lakeside He came to those men who knew Him not. He speaks to us the same word, 'Follow thou Me,' and sets us to the same task which He has to fulfil for our time. He commands. And to those who obey Him, whether they be wise or simple, He will reveal Himself in the toils, the conflicts, the sufferings which they shall pass through in His fellowship, and as an ineffable mystery they shall learn in their own experience who He is."

One school of thought finds it difficult to worship Jesus as Lord because it starts with the pre-sup-position that He cannot have had much more insight or intelligence than those who associated with Him and handed down His sayings (9). There is no reason to doubt the honesty and directness of the persons who hold this view; but the Jesus they reconstruct for us would never have been influential enough in His own day to have been able to bear the weight of the honour of Kurios which the Graeco-Roman world subsequently bestowed upon Him. To regard Christ as speaking to us greater things than even a learned scholar can perfectly comprehend is still the better way of accounting for His undying in-fluence. To treat the story of the rich young ruler as a piece of cold prose, and to make our Lord's answer into a general principle instead of one of the finest snubs ever administered to a self-satisfied bourgeois is to show a lamentable absence of insight. Do we suppose moreover that the Roman Empire would have thought it worth while to make a treaty of surrender with a Jewish prophet whose chief con-tribution to spiritual certainty was a misconception of the course of history such as any ordinary catechumen could have detected? Even the merest child in a Bible-class can understand that the sermon on the mount was spoken not to the crowds but to the inner circle of disciples as an ideal picture of the morals and motives of the citizens of the Kingdom of God; a picture so strange that it staggers us to find that the world has moved even a little in the direction of realising it. The fact remains that we cannot expound the teaching of Christ in the same way as the King's regulations for the Army, and it is idle to try; for Christ put ideas into the world of so flaming and revolutionary a character that so far from having been superseded, they are still too great for our small chilly hearts.

There is no doubt much attraction to orderly minds in the evolutionary idea of an absolute and perfect religion realising itself or being revealed in the end of the time process. But there are distinct objections to such a belief. First of all, the human best is not usually a final but a middle term in a series. The senile is not the highest. Secondly, analogies drawn from biology quite as readily suggest the achievement in religion of a high static position leading to differentiation on a firm level, rather than of indefinite evolution. In the third place, the creative period in religion on a grand scale has to all appearances gone by. "Just as in civilisation great new developments are rare, and it is simply the individual nuances which increase with the working out of the great fundamental schemes, while the activity of the individual diminishes, so it is to a much larger degree in the sphere of religion. With the progress of history the creative religious forces

in the individual become scantier. He is possessed
by ideas which deepen and intensify, and his activity
becomes concentrated more and more on appropriating these great ideas, to which his piety can
only add nuances of emphasis and thought....
There seems little reason to suppose that the future
will show an immeasurable welter of religious pro-
ductivity. It is much more likely that there will be
development on the plateau we have already
reached, and a conflict between already existing
forces as long as our civilisation continues. Then
will come the victory of the highest value, and the
comprehension within it of all reality." (10)

It is sometimes asserted that science is on the
verge of inventing a new religion. "Certainly there
be some that delight in giddiness, and count it a
bondage to fix a belief." Now it would be foolish
to deny that the natural sciences have contributed
nothing to our knowledge of the majesty and
wisdom of God. They have given and are giving us
countless new and marvellous illustrations of His
ways of working. But it is reasonable to ask—do
they give us any single dogma which is fundamentally new, and entirely contradictory of past
religious experience? Are not the religious speculations of men of science virtually those of the greatest
philosophers of antiquity? Language may change
and different details be discussed, but the problems
of transcendence and immanence, of omnipotence
and love, of natural law and freedom, of pluralism
and monism, of the one good God versus dualism
or pessimism; these seem to be eternal. If a creative

revolution should overtake the organised Churches, as it very likely may, it will do so not as something superseding Christ, but as an attempt on the one hand to make the organised expressions of Christianity rather more Christian than they are at present, and on the other hand to penetrate the old spiritual notions of the world with the light of the new knowledge of the external universe and the mind of man. But new knowledge is not the same thing as a new religion. So far, for example, from abolishing all prayer, the findings of modern science lead us away from the paganism of much current liturgical practice back to the real teaching of Jesus upon prayer as a reverent harmonisation of the human will with the divine rule, and a claiming of all those good gifts which a trustworthy deity may be relied upon to give with perfect impartiality. Prof. Leuba concludes his disconcertingly scientific work on the *Psychology of Religious Mysticism* with the unexpected assertion: "It is not a replacement of the religious spirit by science which is indicated here, but the inclusion into religion of the relevant scientific knowledge. The hope of humanity lies in a collaboration of religious idealism with science."

There is a fourth argument, that the postponement of a perfect revelation to the final term of the human series conflicts with the conception of a good and rational God. "On this view," says Prof. Matthews [11], "it is clear that we must wait till the end of history for the complete revelation of God. Not until the drama of humanity is played out can we know how deeply our partial revelations were infected with error, or certainly apprehend the parts we were intended to play. When the last man is tottering to his frozen grave, or when the comet that is to shatter the world is in the sky, only then will the Will of God have been completely revealed. Only when there are no human minds left to know Him and no human wills to obey, will His self-disclosure be accomplished. The end is the one place where revelation is useless, but on this hypothesis it is the one place where it is certain. If theism is true, and wisdom and love in God bear any resemblance to wisdom and love in man, we may be sure that this hypothesis is false." I am not sure myself that I like this particular argument, because unless the revelation Prof. Matthews wants is set forth right at the beginning of the world, there must always be some human lives lived without knowledge of it, while unless the human race were really descended from a single pair, which is so far not proven, the only way in which such necessary knowledge could be fairly distributed would be by its simultaneous publication. It would be quite as unmerciful to deprive the human race of necessary religious knowledge at the beginning of its career as to defer communication till half-way through or to reserve it to the end. If we are going to use the moment of the appearance of Christianity as an argument for accepting it, the most we can say is that it stands central in a period of the earth's history when the creative forces of religion were at their strongest, and that therefore it came, as has often been said, "in the fulness of time," i.e. when things were ready for it. If disease is not the will of the good and merciful God who rules the universe, it is difficult, on the lines of Prof. Matthew's argument, to see why humanity should have had to struggle for many weary centuries before proper methods of medical and surgical treatment could be discovered. One can only suggest that it is the Divine wisdom to let man win his treasures for himself by effort, and to relinquish them into His hands in a sequence the meaning of which our limited though arrogant understanding is unable as yet to explain.

There is no objection to the idea of an absolute and normative point of religion in some period preceding our own. We have neither right to assume nor reason to suppose that a community which uses wireless and can make long excursions in motor-coaches is in a better position to know and obey the will of God than a peasant who drives a bullock cart and gets his news through the group of talkers squatting round the village well. Revelation can hardly depend on the presence or absence of coal or oil, and there is no reason why the decisive and normative event in the history of religion upon this planet should occur in London and New York rather than in Nazareth—or for the matter of that in Epworth or Fenny Drayton.

I do not wish of course to be unsympathetic or indeed anything but modest in the presence of the new learning. For myself, I have never had painfully to discard the old view of the Scriptures, since I cannot remember ever having had any belief about them which gripped me at all, until at the age of fifteen I was instructed in them by a Scotch lay-man who had won distinction for himself rather as a chemist than as a theologian, and knew only the critical method of approach; while our own school of historical research has prevented me from cherishing any picturesque illusions about the early history of the Church. But to those who say: "How can you put your faith in a religious system which seems to us to have grown up in closest unity with almost all the things that the gathering force of empirical investigation of the last 250 years has led us to discard, which stands with belief in a flat earth, a solid sky, a subterranean 'hell,' a geocentric universe, the cosmogony of Genesis, miracles and magic as evidence of Divinity, practically no medical science at all, and almost total ignorance of the real character of the forces of nature by which we are surrounded?"—to such I reply, "If you ask me, I simply challenge you to show that a single one of these things has any connection with the summary of Christ's doctrine which we have just had before us, or with His extraordinary power to win for Himself the loyalty of mankind." Of course it may be objected that the summary is inadequate, and that the accounts of the historical Jesus are con-flicting. But I venture in all humility to challenge both those assertions. It is not common sense to say that the personality of Jesus is not known to us. It simply throbs through all the records we have. Can anyone deny that the real conviction that this personality communicates is in effect what has been stated? For some ecclesiastically minded persons there are no doubt what William James has called "over-beliefs." But the average person is quite content with a good deal less.

The propriety of linking the idea of an absolute and normative religion with an historical individual has been called in question, and we have already tried to give some reasons in its defence. But there is more which can still be said. It does not seem wise to set aside all the speculative thought of mid-Europe upon this matter and merely say that it is unorthodox. The problems created by biblical criticism and kindred studies have touched Christian theology in this island later than elsewhere, but it is idle to reject them and equally idle to refuse to look at what other people have written about them.

Now there is certainly due to Hegel one quite definite method of describing the way in which the person of Jesus may be regarded as central for religion. Hegel saw three great phases in religion: (1) the religion of nature, (2) the religion of spiritual individuality, and (3) absolute religion. Hegel's detailed classification is now obsolete, but his recognition of the fact that Christianity presents something unique which has to be accounted for in a philosophical manner remains as a permanent contribution. Hegel saw, and expressed in his own way that Christianity raised the problem of an absolute religion seriously for the first time, because of its peculiar and distinctive claim to universality, and its remarkable fitness to uphold that claim. We might say, in fact, that mankind without the

teaching of Jesus might have complacently settled
down to the idea of a number of competing races
and religious systems. But the notion of the Kingdom of God has effectively destroyed that possibility.
How then to account for Jesus? Is it His message
about God that is absolute? Or is it His person that
is absolute? Or does His Personality as displayed
in His career constitute the message? That the
general tendency has been to accept this latter
alternative question and to answer it in the affirmative will I suppose be generally admitted. A further
question immediately follows, as to the way in
which that Personality may be properly described.
It is no business of mine to deal in these lectures
at length with the solutions which have been
offered us in recent years of the equation: "Jesus
= Perfect God + Perfect Man," but I will say this
much. I accept the real humanity of our Lord, and
I recognise that the reason why for some centuries
it seemed almost obscure was because men were
conscious to an overwhelming degree that in and
through Him they felt as nowhere else the Presence
and Power of God. Now that was and is an experience and not a theory, and it is a sound scientific
maxim that any object is the sum of its functions.
"When we can sum up the functions of any force
we understand it about as well as there is any use
in understanding it at all." It is not to the point
to ask whether we can find some measure of this
force elsewhere than in Jesus—in the saints for
example, or in Pagan prophets, or in the good
qualities which endear to us the ordinary human

beings of our acquaintance. Very likely we can, and that is going to influence our theory of the person of Christ. But the point is: Can we find God *as much* anywhere as in Jesus? Is it not true that "the best hope of mankind is that the living God is in Jesus and through Him may flow down through all the secret runnels of the race?" (12)

What shall we say about the future? The over-laying of the picture of our Lord by bad science and false history has unhappily led many to misjudge and misunderstand Him. The result has been that not a few have raised the question of the possibility of one or more new religions developing in the future (13). It must be confessed that the prospects for such developments do not look particularly bright. Religions grow and are not artificially in-vented. There is no evidence that the great creative period in religion lies in front of us. The Semites and the Europeans are sceptical and old, and have lost self-confidence. From them we can look for no new religion. The greatest propagandist force in the world to-day is American Protestantism with the American dollar behind it. There will be a tremendous fight between fundamentalism and moderate liberalism, and I think the latter will win in the long run. But the white man is a diminishing factor in America as elsewhere. Six out of seven citizens of the British Empire are coloured. It is not mere extravagance of fancy when Dr Harpf pictures a negro or mulatto ruling at Washington, and Asiatics in high office in London, Paris and Berlin in 400 years' time. But the races which are on the rise show a tendency, in so far as their progressive men remain religious, to develop a faith founded in some way upon the person of Jesus. On the other hand, I do not see how any thoughtful person can suppose that the main types of organised Christianity as they exist to-day can effectively survive much longer. They depend too largely upon a compromise with the lower forms of pre-Christian religion to be able to withstand the attacks of science, and their God is still much more Zeus Pantocrator than the trustworthy and philocosmic but self-limited parent of the gospel teaching. It is significant that the rising school in the Church of England is turning men's thoughts to the inner life of harmonious communion, of "infinite love in ordinary intercourse," rather than to the organised cultus with its attendant dangers of adulatory worship.

I venture to conclude with two verdicts put forth by Troeltsch in his essays, not, it is true, representing his latest opinion, but as it seems to me a more balanced judgment than the one to which he inclined in the last two years of his life, after the war had driven him more and more into individualism:

From the facts as they stand a completely convincing proof cannot be deduced. We can only say that as far as can be seen every religious force of the highest order depends on the Christian religion for its final sanction. Beyond this point, proofs come to an end, and we have left only that personal conviction, that sure confidence which no individual can analyse, however deeply he may feel it, that a new and higher religion is utterly improbable. . . . Although Christianity succeeded other religions as a fundamentally new step forward, yet all the widening and deepening of spiritual life

which has taken place since has been achieved on the basis
of Christianity, and has brought with it nothing fundamentally new....The essential conception of the Absolute
is as that of something lying beyond history. Present
Christianity we cannot and dare not therefore regard as
absolute changeless truth in its final form. Its very simplest
teaching is that the individual is admitted into the Fellowship of the Divine Spirit, in order that he may be guided
into truth and receive knowledge of things that are to come
and so face the future with courage and firm creative fearlessness. But the life of Christ is of absolute value, because
faith regards it as the central permanent and decisive up-
lifting of the religious level, the setting up of a broad plateau
on which man can dwell if he will, though on it he can if
he will rove far afield (14).

And once again, emphasising the fact that in the
vision of God given us by Jesus we are face to face
with what may be called if we like an intuition or
revelation of the character and purpose of the
Divine—of love and self-sacrificing service, of truth
and beauty and goodness, of a creative and holy
activity fashioning a fellowship or commonwealth
of free spirits—Troeltsch says:

The history of spiritual religion is the tracing out of a
chain, to the final link of which we ourselves have not yet
attained. In the vision which we have experienced we have
stretched forward in expectation to that final link, and in
the faltering progress of the Christian Church we are now
gradually inch by inch realising in fact what we have
stretched forward to in expectation (15).

In times of doubts and questionings, when our belief is perplexed by new learning, new teaching, new thought; when our faith is strained by creeds, by doctrines, by mysteries beyond our understanding; give us the faithfulness of learners and the courage of believers in Thee: give us boldness to examine, and faith to trust all truth; patience and insight to master difficulties; stability to hold fast our traditions with enlightened interpretations, to admit all fresh truth made known to us, and in times of trouble to grasp new knowledge and to combine it loyally and honestly with the old. Save us and help us we humbly beseech Thee, O Lord. Amen.

A Prayer by BISHOP RIDDING.

EPILOGUE

THE FUTURE OF ORGANISED
CHRISTIANITY*

They shall teach no more every man his neighbour and every man his brother saying, Know the Lord: for they shall all know me, from the least of them unto the greatest of them, saith the Lord.
                                        Jeremiah xxxi, 34 ff.

NOT long ago, a certain professor asked a thoughtful undergraduate whether in the generations to come there would be any clergy at all. He considered for a moment and then replied: "Oh! yes, but then some day everybody will be a clergyman." Now I hope that you feel the interest and importance of that answer as much as I do. I doubt whether the speaker had even so much as subconsciously drawn his remark from the text which I have chosen, but it is plain that both embody the same conception, namely, a state of human society in which the bond between God and man is so close, and the commerce between heaven and earth so free, natural, and un-interrupted that there is no need for church or temple, and no demand for the services of a pro-fessional clergy. The human race, according to this conception, will eventually come to regard the whole world as equally in all its parts the temple of God, and each individual will attain to such a high standard of spiritual development that he will be able to claim as his own what the mystics call the unitive life, and to say in very truth: "I know Him in whom I have believed."

* Preached in Queens' College Chapel, Cambridge, during the Michaelmas term, 1924.

This notion, occurring in the writings of Jeremiah nearly 600 years before Christ, impresses us as being what is commonly called "advanced thought." We feel it to be a dream of the future falling into much the same category as the imaginative pictures of the world of 31,000 A.D. in Mr Bernard Shaw's "Methuselah" cycle. Even to-day we do not find it either an easy or a congenial task to visualise such a condition of religion. Yet before all things it needs to be remembered that this notion of a sublime personal relationship stands very nearly central in the teaching of our Lord Jesus Christ. Although during his lifetime he inflicted no actual boycott upon the Jewish temple and its sacrifices, his message of the Kingdom of God and of eternal life as present and open to all, and of prayer as a natural and intimate relation between the child of God and the Heavenly Father are a direct development of the idea contained in the words of Jeremiah.

But this pure and spiritual teaching proved itself too mighty for the followers of those who received it. It has ever been the case that human beings are unequally endowed with a natural faculty for knowing God. Mankind is mostly made up of a few mystics, a limited number of real secularists, and between the two a mass of feebly and intermittently religious persons, the "dim common populations" who form the vast majority and who sway as it were between the head and the tail. The personality of Christ impressed itself, as indeed it could not fail to have impressed itself, on the world of late antiquity, but that world was made up of just the very elements we have described. The average population in Antioch, Alexandria, Constantinople or Rome, proved itself incapable of responding to an idea for which it was hardly prepared. It demanded a priesthood, a sacrificial system, an authoritative creed, and a dual standard of morals, for monastic orders as well as for ordinary people. Perhaps we may say that God in his mercy allowed it these things because of the hardness of men's hearts.

It was not therefore until nearly sixteen centuries later that any widespread attempt was embarked upon which had for its aim the popularising of *personal* religion as conceived by Christ. While nobody can deny its sporadic existence in Christendom at an earlier date, it must be generally admitted that one of the great aims of what we call the Reformation as a whole was to try to make personal religion universal. Every ploughboy was to be able to read the classic documents of Christianity in his own language. Public prayers also were to be in the vernacular. Salvation, even if still thought of as future, was to be ensured by a simple act of faith, instead of by an elaborate system of devotional exercises conducted by officials. The act of sacramental communion, shorn of Pagan accretions, was to be, as far as possible, frequent and universal. Intermediaries between the soul and God, whether sacrificing priests or interceding saints, were declared unnecessary. From that time onward until now the aim and watchword of Evangelical Protestantism has been personal knowledge of God in

Christ as Saviour and Friend, by every individual from the least to the greatest.

But once again there has been a falling short in the working out of the ideal. A large mass of Europeans actually showed themselves at the time of the Reformation unwilling to give up the older system. They liked to have their prayers said for them by someone else and to practise their religion by proxy. Even those who called themselves Protestants preferred for the most part to take what their minister or Bible said to them about God, and not to think too much about it for themselves. At Geneva they even submitted to the construction of a new and rigid church polity. In this perhaps they showed a certain degree of commonsense, since the efforts of thoroughgoing Protestants who exalted private judgment to an extravagant degree were not on the whole encouraging. Many men (as has been said) preferred the older system, which made fewer demands on the individual, and amongst ourselves there has been a considerable reaction in favour of it in recent years. Indeed, if we are to have a church polity at all, there is much to be said for adopting one which has behind it the glories of antiquity and the treasures of art wherewith to enrich its public cultus.

And yet, there is the ideal, and we can see to-day that it has not slipped out of the mind of humanity. It still attracts. Men and women still feel that it is the right thing at which to aim. It manifests itself to-day in a variety of forms, some of them perhaps rather strange ones. First of all there is the great interest, sustained now for nearly a generation, in mystical religion and the psychology of religious experience. Then there is the decline in the fashion of hearing sermons as a matter of routine, and still more striking the change in the observance of Sunday as well as of Christmas Day and Good Friday and other holy days of obligation. I think further that we must place in the same group the decline in the number of candidates for the ministry. Let me, if you will, develop these points a little.

It seems, in the first place, that while personal religion in isolated instances has often flourished quite as much among persons of meagre education as among highly educated individuals, it makes on the whole such an imperious demand upon the individual that it can only become general among those who have sufficiently trained and disciplined characters to cultivate it. The growth of education provides favourable soil for personal religion because it develops self-reliance. A vicarious ministry postulates an illiterate or ignorant, untrained, and dependent laity. Even for the Roman Catholic aristocracy, the ideal as outlined by Mgr. Talbot in a now notorious phrase was: "To hunt, to shoot, to entertain," and not to meddle in church affairs. Yet surely it is a good thing to make great demands upon the individual for personal sacrifice and intelligent interest.

It is certain that the decline in the hearing of sermons is due quite as much to educational and other facilities as to any fall in the standard of preaching or waning of interest in religion. A limited

number of outstanding preachers who possess more
than average insight and have a real message of
their own to deliver are and always will be sure of
a hearing, and their sermons will probably in the
future be more and more widely broadcasted; but
the average clergyman of to-day must be aware that
his hearers, if in earnest, are in almost as favourable
a position to know and proclaim the will of God as
he is, and the whole tendency at the present time
is to popularise religious thought in small booklets
and cheap editions of standard theological works.

It is hard to believe that the decline in church-
going and in the special observance of Sunday is
due in the main to secular interests or anti-religious
feeling. It is true that these latter find in it their
opportunity, but for the origin of the decline we
may not unreasonably look to the gradual growth
and development of the liberal spirit in religion.
St Paul's argument about the observance and non-
observance of days was applied no doubt in the
sixteenth century to saints' days, vigils, and church
seasons. I have heard it used in regard to the last
by a Baptist maid-servant arguing with an Anglican
friend. But why stop there? Why not make all
the days of our life equally a matter of religious
observance? Why select Sunday more than Monday?
The Catholic has his daily Mass and the Evangelical
his daily prayer meeting. Why keep one day specially
sacred, and so imply the secularity of the rest? I am
profoundly sure that this kind of argument lurks
at the back of the minds of many of the younger
generation.

So too with the Ministry. Many men are ceasing to be ordained, not because they are irreligious or selfish, or even because they feel themselves unfitted for ordination, but because they do not see exactly how the ministry to-day provides them with a specific whole-time occupation. Various types of social service which used to be performed by the clergy in the course of their parochial duties are now provided either by the State or by employers of labour. Young men who recognise what is known as the priesthood of the laity no longer feel it necessary to be ordained in order to fulfil duties which seem to them simply part of that priesthood. They see laymen allowed to preach and give religious addresses and even to conduct parts of public worship. As doctors, schoolmasters, welfare-workers in factories, employers of labour, or scoutmasters, they find they can render Christian service, and they react more and more against the idea that religious work is specially connected with one particular calling—that of the clergyman. There is also a growing dislike of being paid to be a clergyman. Quite a number of army chaplains at the end of the Great War favoured the idea of earning their living in some other way than the official ministry and so of being able to give their services gratis as pastors, preachers or conductors of public worship. The taunt of being professional Christians is no idle one, as we clergy have unhappily occasion to observe, and even if it be legitimate "to live of the Gospel," there is much to be urged in favour of earning one's keep independently.

It seems therefore that in spite of the opportunity which times of change give to those who seek in unsettlement an excuse for carelessness and indifference, we may justly regard the altering attitude towards institutional religion as on the whole a sign of progress in thought. Perhaps after all we are standing in the midst of the process of that further Reformation for which some, among others the late Lord Morley, have wished and hoped.

And yet there is another side to the matter. The spiritual life has ever to struggle for its existence. The flesh lusteth against the spirit and the spirit against the flesh and these are contrary the one to the other so that we cannot do the things that we desire to do.

(1) It is very questionable whether in the face of worldliness and moral turpitude religion can maintain its values unless those who prize them hold together in an intense federal unity. And that means inevitably a Church, and whole time leaders and specialists, and shepherding of souls and fellowship in action. There are the many weaker brethren to be considered, and in no other department of life, and certainly not in this, are we yet able to dispense with the leader. The Church exists mainly in this world because she is militant; and a successful army is not a mere crowd of well-meaning individuals with a common intention.

(2) Men, like ants and bees, are biologically social creatures. That eminent Frenchman was undoubtedly right who spoke somewhere of the

distinction between "la dévotion étroite" and "la grande religion." While we do well to recognise the Presence of God in things that are homely and simple, we make a false antithesis if we go on to ignore or to deny that Presence in the magnificent and the sublime. Strip away quite rightly as much as you can of the cumbersome organisation and complex and often meaningless ceremonial which readily accumulate round all social institutions, and even then you will not be free to dispense entirely with the institutions themselves. Fellowship counts for much. Team work is able to yield results which are the product rather than the sum of co-operation, and generally surpass anything that the individual is able to achieve. Corporate worship and meditation may be used quite as much to intensify religious earnestness as to depress religious standards. The individual, great as are his possibilities, has yet that narrowness about him which is the price of being an individual. He must pool his private experience, that in the greater reservoir of universal experience it may find its own level. I believe it to be the Will of God that the human expression of religion should find at least as great heights in combination as in individual effort—perhaps greater heights. In Bach's Mass in B Minor the mighty Sanctus is quite as important as any of the intricately wrought solos; yet the choir and orchestra by whom it is sounded forth are no mere aggregate of individuals functioning independently. This analogy may be applied to the work of the Church.

Although perhaps in the future we may see no

inconsiderable increase in the number of clergy of the unpaid type, and a still greater increase in individual devotion and personal mysticism, I still think that for the above reasons we shall not be able to dispense with efficient clergy who give their whole time to the work of the ministry, and I still think that whether its function be that of shepherding individuals or of leading in team work, the ministry is still as great and grand a calling as ever. The vast majority of mankind find that sustained religious effort is difficult, and their personalities tend to express themselves rhythmically, so that their attention to matters of vital importance ebbs and flows like a tide, or swings to and fro like a pendulum. They need much shepherding in the long process of life, and it is the function of the clergy to act as leaders and shepherds.

The business of the clergy is to stand to their people as Christ the Good Shepherd stands to humanity as a whole. It is a most sacred and difficult relationship to maintain, and the call to it is a very solemn one. But it is neither trivial nor ignoble. It is. at least "a man's job," and those who are called to it cannot train themselves too carefully or too thoroughly. Moreover, if an orchestra needs a conductor, a church certainly needs a leader, so that the function of the priest or elder or steward of divine mysteries, as the leader of its corporate life, is easy to comprehend.

If fewer men are seen to be adopting the ministerial career to-day, we may assign that fact to one or more of three causes. It may either be that many

are resisting the call, or that many are honestly
deterred from responding through perfectly con-
scientious scruples about accepting work in which
the present rate of pay can hardly provide any of
those who lack unearned increment with the possibility of being able either to help their parents in
their old age, or to marry and maintain a wife except
in a state of drudgery and meanness, or to educate
suitably any children that may be born of such a
marriage. Or, in the third place, the shortage may
be due to the fact that God is actually calling fewer
men to ordination, because He wishes the Church
to change her methods and desires fewer and better
professional whole-time clergy, and more of the other
sort—those who are unpaid and earning their living
independently of their sacred functions.

But the real defect at present lies, it would seem,
in the fact that not enough men learn to think of
the Christian ministry as one of leadership, and so
the ministry loses many a strong character, and is,
I think, rendered unattractive to just the men who
are needed, through a misunderstanding of its nature
and aims. It badly needs strong characters, men
whose love of truth is greater than that of party,
who will not be hampered by prejudice or partial
views, and who are prepared to give the energy of
their best years to ordinary solid pastoral work,
which is required at present more than anything
else, alike in our villages and in our large centres of
population. Such work, lovingly undertaken, will
be found to be its own reward: but those who undertake it must ever keep before them the great ideal,

that ideal in which each individual soul is raised to its full spiritual height.

They shall all know me, saith the Lord, from the greatest even to the least.

Ye shall be perfect even as your Father which is in heaven is perfect.

Till we all attain unto the unity of the faith and of the knowledge of the Son of God, unto a full-grown man, unto the measure of the stature of the fulness of Christ.

The vision truly is not for many days, but that it is a right vision, who can doubt?

NOTES TO LECTURE I

(1) R. H. THOULESS. *Introduction to the Psychology of Religion.* Cambridge, 1923, p. 4.

(2) JUNG. Quoted by W. B. Selbie, *Introduction to Religious Psychology*, Oxford, 1924; and again in *Psychological Types*, 1923, viz.:

> "This libido accumulation animates images.... Here is the source of the God-idea. For our psychology...God is but a function of the unconscious.... The divine effect springs from our own inner self."

(3) SIMMEL. Quoted by Troeltsch, *Gesammelte Schriften*, 1911, p. 91, "Weltanschauung." S. is described as "one of the acutest observers of our day."

> "In der Beilage der Vossischen Zeitung schrieb Simmel...die moderne Wissenschaft habe in der Tat jeden Gedanken an Gott und an Göttliches Wirken unmöglich gemacht aber sie habe natürlich die Tatsache des religiösen Gefühls selbst nicht beseitigen können. Dieses liege als eine besondere Zuständlichkeit und Stimmung im Menschen... man müsse es nur als einen seelischen Schwingungszustand fassen, ohne auf Gott und Gottesgedanken zu reflektieren, eine Religion ohne Gott und ohne Gemeinschaft...."

So also Santayana in his philosophical writings.

(4) Cf. Dr WILLIAM BROWN, quoted by Selbie, p. 296; see also Prof. D. MIALL EDWARDS: *Philosophy of Religion*, 1924, ch. VII:

> "But the fact is, the psychologist who assumes that since all the phenomena of religion can be explained in terms of mental processes which he can analyse, therefore religion can be proved to be an illusion, will find himself in an awkward predicament. For in the same way the objective reality of the world around us can be denied. For the psychological analysis of the experience of sense-perception discovers nothing but a subjective process and finds no room for any object to improve upon it. But it is surely absurd to think that by analysing the experiencing mind we are explaining away the reality of the object experienced. This is a fallacy into which the psychologist naturally falls whenever

he forgets that a psychology of the experiencING process is not the same thing as a philosophy of experienceD reality. The question of the validity of experience or the nature of reality is the province of philosophy, not of psychology. To reduce religious ideas to symbols of subconscious desires is not to prove them illusory, for it leaves the question still open whether the universe does or does not correspond with our desires. To trace the psychological history of a belief does not dispense with the question of its truth or falsity, which must be answered on other grounds than those of its origin or history. It is a philosophical commonplace that lowly origin must not be allowed to prejudice the validity or value of the final result."

Cf. also Thouless, *op. cit.* p. 138 f.:

"It is possible that the Freudians who insist that it (infantile sexuality) is a factor of such importance are in the position of botanists who, having dug round the roots of an oak tree, have discovered the remains of the acorn from which it grew, and insist that in this alone lies all the significance of the oak; and that the other scientists, who spend their lives in the investigation of the structure of the tree itself, the artists who rejoice in its beauty, and the carpenters who make use of its wood, are all alike living in a fool's paradise, because they have not realised that the oak is a decayed acorn and nothing more."

(5) W. K. Wright. *A Student's Philosophy of Religion.* 1922.
(6) Bernard Bosanquet. *Contemporary Philosophy.* 1921, p. 67.
(7) In *Eternal Life.* 1912.
(8) Bryce. *Modern Democracies.* 1920.
(9) Dr Bernard Hart. *The Psychology of Insanity.* Camb. Univ. Press, p. 71 and indeed chs. v, vi, and vii in general.
(10) *Manifesto of the Communist Party,* 1847.
Three extracts may be given, (1) from the introduction; (2), (3) from the Manifesto itself:
(1) "The 'Manifesto' being our joint production, I* consider myself bound to state that the fundamental
* *i.e.* Engels.

proposition which forms its nucleus, belongs to Marx. That proposition is: that in every historical epoch, the prevailing mode of economic production and exchange, and the social organisation necessarily following from it form the basis on which it is built up, and from which alone can be explained, the political and intellectual history of that epoch; that consequently the whole history of mankind (since the dissolution of primitive tribal society, holding land in common ownership) has been a history of class struggles, contests between exploiting and exploited, ruling and oppressed classes; that the history of these class struggles forms a series of evolution in which, now-a-days, a stage has been reached where the exploited and oppressed class— the proletariat—cannot attain its emancipation from the sway of the exploiting and ruling class— the bourgeoisie—without, at the same time, and once and for all, emancipating society at large from all exploitation, oppression, class-distinctions and class struggles.

"This proposition, which, in my opinion, is destined to do for history what Darwin's theory has done for biology, we both of us had been gradually approaching for some years before 1845. How far I had independently progressed towards it is best shown by my *Condition of the Working Class in England* (b). But when I again met Marx at Brussels, in spring, 1845, he had it ready worked out, and put it before me, in terms almost as clear as those in which I have stated it here."

(2) "In the conditions of the proletariat, those of the old society at large are already virtually swamped. The proletarian is without property; his relation to his wife and children has no longer anything in common with the bourgeois family-relations; modern industrial labour, modern subjection to capital, the same in England as in France, in America as in Germany, has stripped him of every trace of national character. Law, morality, religion, are to him so many bourgeois prejudices, behind which lurk in ambush just as many bourgeois interests."

(3) "When the ancient world was in its last throes, the ancient religions were overcome by Christianity.

When Christian ideas succumbed in the 18th century to rationalist ideas, feudal society fought its death battle with the then revolutionary bourgeoisie. The ideas of religious liberty and freedom of conscience merely gave expression to the sway of free competition within the domain of knowledge.

"'Undoubtedly,' it will be said, 'religious, moral, philosophical and juridical ideas have been modified in the course of historical development. But religion, morality, philosophy, political science, and law, constantly survived this change.'

"'There are besides, eternal truths, such as Freedom, Justice, etc., that are common to all states of society. But Communism abolishes eternal truths, it abolishes all religion, and all morality, instead of constituting them on a new basis; it therefore acts in contradiction to all past historical experience.'

"What does this accusation reduce itself to? The history of all past society has consisted in the development of class antagonisms, antagonisms that assumed different forms at different epochs.

"But whatever form they may have taken, one fact is common to all past ages, viz.: the exploitation of one part of society by another. No wonder, then, that the social consciousness of past ages, despite all the multiplicity and variety it displays, moves within certain common forms, or general ideas, which cannot completely vanish except with the total disappearance of class antagonisms.

"The Communist's is the most radical rupture with traditional property-relations; no wonder that its development involves the most radical rupture with traditional ideas."

(11) From a pamphlet published in Glasgow, 1921.

(12), (13) *Towards a Communist Programme.* 1921. Sec. 2.H.

(14) See, for example, *Resolutions and Theses of the Fourth Congress of the Communist International*, Moscow, 1922.

(15) MORE. *Utopia.* Temple Classics. 1901, p. 139.

(16) F. JOLLIVET-CASTELOT. *L'idée communiste.* Édition de la Rose et Croix. 19, Rue St-Jean à Douai, Nord.

(17), (18) BACON. *Meditationes Sacrae X.*

(19) *Essays of a Biologist.* Final chapter.

(20) KARL MARX. *Das Kapital.* Vol. I, ch. X and also chs. XXV and XXVII.

The whole of this chapter should be read by all clergy and ordination candidates, in order to understand the origin and propagation of class bitterness. It is past rather than present iniquities that rankle.

The following extracts from Engels' preface, showing what he thought about the book he was editing, may be interesting. (It is hard to believe that this was written as long ago as 1886):

"*Das Kapital* is often called, on the continent, 'the Bible of the working class.' That the conclusions arrived at in this work are daily more and more becoming the fundamental principles of the great working class movement, not only in Germany and Switzerland, but in France, in Holland and Belgium, in America, and even in Italy and Spain; that everywhere the working class more and more recognises, in these conclusions, the most adequate expression of its condition and of its aspirations, nobody acquainted with that movement will deny. And in England, too, the theories of Marx, even at this moment, exercise a most powerful influence upon the socialist movement which is spreading in the ranks of the 'cultured' people no less than in those of the working class. But that is not all. The time is rapidly approaching when a thorough examination of England's economic position will impose itself as an irresistible national necessity. The working of the industrial system of this country, impossible without a constant and rapid extension of production, and therefore of markets, is coming to a dead stop. Free trade has exhausted its resources; even Manchester doubts this its quondam economic gospel. Foreign industry, rapidly developing, stares English production in the face everywhere, not only in protected, but also in neutral markets, and even on this side of the Channel. While the productive power increases in a geometric, the extension of the markets proceeds at best in an arithmetic ratio. The decennial cycle of stagnation, prosperity, over production and crisis, ever recurrent from 1825 to 1867, seems indeed to have run its course; but only to land us in the slough of despond of a permanent and chronic depression."

"The sighed for period of prosperity will not come; as often as we seem to perceive its heralding symptoms, so often do they again vanish into air. Meanwhile, each succeeding winter brings up afresh the great question, 'what to do with the unemployed,' but while the number of the unemployed keeps swelling from year to year, there is nobody to answer that question; and we can almost calculate the moment when the unemployed, losing patience, will take their own fate into their own hands. Surely, at such a moment, the voice ought to be heard of a man whose whole theory is the result of a lifelong study of the economic history and condition of England, and whom that study led to the conclusion that, at least in Europe, England is the only country where the inevitable social revolution might be effected entirely by peaceful and legal means. He certainly never forgot to add that he hardly expected the English ruling classes to submit, without a 'pro-slavery rebellion,' to this peaceful and legal rebellion."

Author's preface, p. xxx, showing the attitude of Marx towards metaphysics:

"My dialectic method is not only different from the Hegelian, but is its direct opposite. To Hegel, the life-process of the human brain, i.e. the process of thinking, which, under the name of 'the Idea' he even transforms into an independent subject, is the demiurgos of the real world, and the real world is only the external, phenomenal form of 'the Idea.' With me, on the contrary, the ideal is nothing more than the material world reflected by the human mind, and translated into forms of thought.

"The mystifying side of Hegelian dialectic I criticised nearly thirty years ago, at a time when it was still the fashion. But just as I was working at the first volume of *Das Kapital*, it was the good pleasure of the peevish, arrogant, mediocre Ἐπίγονοι who now talk large in cultured Germany, to treat Hegel in the same way as the brave Moses Mendelssohn in Lessing's time treated Spinoza, i.e. as a 'dead dog.' I therefore openly avowed myself the pupil of that

mighty thinker, and even here and there, in the
chapter on the theory of value, coquetted with the
modes of expression peculiar to him. The mystifica-
tion which dialectic suffers in Hegel's hands, by no
means prevents him from being the first to present
its general form of working in a comprehensive and
conscious manner. With him it is standing on its
head. It must be turned right side up again, if you
would discover the rational kernel within the
mystical shell.

"In its mystified form, dialectic became the fashion
in Germany, because it seemed to transfigure and
to glorify the existing state of things. In its rational
form it is a scandal and abomination to bourgeoisdom
and its doctrinaire professors because it includes in
its comprehension and affirmative recognition of
the existing state of things, at the same time also,
the recognition of the negation of that state, of its
inevitable breaking up; because it regards every
historically developed social form as in fluid movement, and therefore takes into account its transient
nature not less than its momentary existence;
because it lets nothing impose upon it, and is in its
essence critical and revolutionary.

"The contradictions inherent in the movement of
capitalist society impress themselves upon the
practical bourgeois most strikingly in the changes
of the periodic cycle, through which modern industry
runs, and whose crowning point is the universal
crisis. That crisis is once again approaching, although
as yet in its preliminary stage; and by the universality
of its theatre and the intensity of its action it will
drum dialectics even into the heads of the mushroom-
upstarts of the new, holy Prusso-German empire."

Remember that it was Marx who said in 1867 (author's
preface): "The English Established Church will more
readily pardon an attack on 38 of its 39 articles than
on $\frac{1}{39}$ of its income."

(21) MARX. *Op. cit.* vol. I, ch. xxv, p. 625.
(22) J. NEVILLE FIGGIS. *Churches in the Modern State.*
Longmans, 1913.
(23) TROELTSCH. *Atheistische Ethik.* Gesammelte Schriften,
p. 557.
(24) AUGUSTINE. *Confessions,* IV, 14, 21.

(25) Dr HERBERT GRAY in a speech made at the Examination Hall, Cambridge, November, 1924.

(26) From a Communist Pamphlet addressed to agricultural labourers. Cf. also the following, by a Socialist Councillor at West Ham, Jan. 1924:

"We (the Socialist Sunday School movement) are not opposed to religion. Neither are we supporting it. We are simply cutting out religion. Our Socialist idea of a universal brotherhood is more important than God or Jesus Christ or any religion."

(27) In justice to the Comintern, it must be noted that the colour bar is explicitly abolished. See *Resolutions and Theses*, etc. as above, p. 84:

"The Comintern will fight for race equality of the negro with the white people," etc.

(28) J. ARTHUR THOMSON. *Gifford Lectures*, vol. II, ch. "Disharmonies and Shadows." Also *The Bible of Nature*, ch. IV, "The Evolution of Organisms," concluding paragraphs.

(29) FOSDICK. *The Modern Use of the Bible*. S.C.M. 1924.

NOTE BY THE AUTHOR ON
"SECULARISM AND SOCIAL REFORM"

While I do not wish to write a separate essay on this subject, I think it is necessary to make some reference to the objection which is often urged against the advocacy of social reform by Christians, namely that it tends to secularise Christianity. I cannot help noticing that this objection has always so far proceeded from those who are themselves quite free from the discomforts which are attacked by social reform. The argument against secularising Christianity by making it concern itself with the comfort of people's bodies rather than with the salvation of their souls would be very much stronger if it came from poor persons, and this unfortunately is not the case. It is, of course, perfectly true that the possession of a moderate standard of comfort need not necessarily foster a reverence for spiritual values. Nevertheless, it is the experience of all who have had much to do with pastoral work that the religious consciousness flourishes most in those communities where there is neither squalid poverty nor extreme riches. If the prospect of a uniformly middle class

world shocks some people, I can only point out that
it is the ideal towards which the whole policy of the
world, both educational and economic, is tending.
The society of the future seems likely to contain a
smaller population with no excessively rich persons,
and if some regulation of the birth-rate be introduced,
no very poor persons. When, therefore, Lord Hugh
Cecil asks whether the Christian social reformer has
any idea as to limiting the standard of human comfort,
my reply would be: "No, if it is a question of the
precise figure; yes, if it is a matter of moderation
and of avoiding extremes." I should like to see the
possession of really large incomes confined to those
persons who either as administrators or in some other
capacity are thought by the community to be deserving
of a rather higher standard of comfort than the
normal. Such would be, for example, the creative
musician, the research student, and certain classes of
professional men such as judges. The right to pass on
by will the enjoyment of such incomes of course raises
difficulties. But if the suggestion does not seem too
extravagant, I would venture to suggest some kind
of inspection of the hereditary possessors of wealth
by chosen representatives of the community; con-
fiscation to follow if the report was unsatisfactory.
This is surely no more unreasonable than the periodic
renewal, after examination or report, of college scholar-
ships or fellowships at some Universities. That the
hereditary possession of a standard of wealth which is
above the average is productive in certain cases
(though not in many) of valuable types of human
beings cannot reasonably be denied, but the world
of the future will certainly not be able to afford the
unrestricted enjoyment of such hereditary advantages.
And then, finally, having established a moderate
standard for human life, society will still remain
powerless to compel its members to cultivate the
highest values. It will only have created conditions
favourable to such cultivation. There is nothing (as
we already see) in the conditions of a so-called middle
class world which can compel anyone to be musical,
metaphysical, religious, courteous, moral, unselfish, or
devoted to good art or great literature. It is only
the favourable conditions which can be guaranteed.
But I would point out that the tendency of modern

thought (though that of course may be mistaken) is to conceive of the whole external universe as one system rather than two, and to think nobly of the material saeculum instead of depreciating it. Is not the world, rightly understood, the revelation and expression of the Invisible Spirit whom we symbolise as God, and is not perhaps he who disdains social reform as outside the province of the Christian minister really a Manichee?

NOTES TO LECTURE II

(1) Prof. W. S. URQUHART, of Calcutta University. *Pantheism and the Value of Life*. Epworth Press, 1919. Ch. II, p. 25.

(2) ALLANSON PICTON. *The Religion of the Universe*. Macmillans, 1910.

(3) Quoted in Urquhart, p. 15.

(4) URQUHART, p. 16.

(5) JULIAN HUXLEY. In *The Outline of Science*, Newnes, 1923. Ch. XIX.

(6) Mrs EDDY. Sermon on "Christian Healing" at Boston. Edition 1917, p. 10.

"God is all and in all; that finishes the question of a good and bad side to existence."

Mrs Eddy, however, in her book *Science and Health*, p. 335, denies that she is a pantheist.

(7) *Dionysius the Areopagite: the Divine Names, and the Mystical Theology*. Translated, with notes, by Rev. C. E. Rolt, and published in 1920 by S.P.C.K.

(8) The following is a list of Mr TRINE's writings:

What all the World's a Seeking. London, 1898. 3 editions.

Every Living Creature. 1899.

In Tune with the Infinite. 1900. 21 editions.

Character-building through Power.

In the Fire of the Heart. 2 editions.

The Land of Living Men. 1911.

The New Alinement of Life. 1913.

My Philosophy and my Religion. 1921.

(9) Prof. KIRSOPP LAKE. *The Stewardship of Faith*. Ch. VI, p. 141.

(10) The last chapter of *Outspoken Essays*, Series I.

(11) HERRMANN VON KEYSERLING. *Das Reisetagebuch eines Philosophs.*
(12) STEFFEN. In *Encycl. Die Religion in Geschichte und Gegenwart.* Article "Buddhismus."
(13) NICHOLSON. *Studies in Islamic Mysticism.* Camb. Univ. Press.
(14) Quoted in *Mysticism*, by EVELYN UNDERHILL, 4th edition, 1912, p. 120.
(15) For a more detailed summary see Prof. MIALL EDWARDS, *Philosophy of Religion.* Hodder and Stoughton, 1924, ch. VIII.
(16) Prof. BISSETT PRATT. *The Religions of India.* Chapter on Buddhism.
(17) URQUHART. Book 3, ch. I.
(18) URQUHART. Book 3, ch. I.
(19) EDDY. Sermon previously quoted.
(20) HOPKINS. *Origin and Evolution of Religion.* 1923, p. 21. What the Hindu actually said was:

> "This is mere matter of intelligence. I, being completely devil-upped, worship only myself, but conform out of liberality to popular superstitions. My wife, lacking intelligence, and not being devil-upped, worships bare image."

(21) Quoted in the *Monist*, 1922.
(22) *Meditations.* Book v, chs. IX and X. Prof. Urquhart's quotation would seem to be a paraphrase. The actual quotation as given in Casaubon's translation, 1634, is:

> "In such obscurity, and impurity of things: in such and so continual a flux both the substances and time; both of the motions themselves and things moved; what it is that we can fasten upon; either to honour and respect especially; or seriously and studiously to seek after; I cannot so much as conceive. For indeed they are things contrary. Thou must comfort thyself in the expectation of thy natural dissolution, and in the meantime not grieve at the delay."

(23) *Meditations.* Book v, ch. XXIII.

> "And if they will not suffer thee, then mayest thou leave thy life rather than thy calling, but so as one that doth not think himself any ways wronged. Only as one would say, here is a smoke; I will out of it."

(24) 1 Corinthians, xv, 28.
(25) John, xvii, 23.
(26) CHARLES WESLEY. Hymn attached to John Wesley's sermon on "Christian Perfection."
(27) Evening hymn by JOHN KEBLE.
(28) Hymn by CHARLES WESLEY.
(29), (30) Quoted by Underhill in *Mysticism*, p. 104.
(31) Sir CHARLES ELIOT. *Hinduism and Buddhism*, pp. 314 and 316.
(32) URQUHART, p. 624.
(33) C. DELISLE BURNS. "History and Philosophy." In *The Monist*. July, 1922. See also TROELTSCH, *Der Historismus und seine Probleme*, Kap. IV, Sec. 3, "Das Problem einer objektiven Periodisierung."
(34) BURKITT. *Comment and Criticism*. May, 1914.
(35) SCHWEITZER. *Christianity and the Religion of the World*, p. 72.
(36) Quoted in Urquhart, p. 700.
(37) FRANCIS THOMPSON. *Essay on Shelley*.
(38) Cf. R. S. SLEIGH. *The Sufficiency of Christianity*, final chapter, and also C. C. J. WEBB, *Gifford Lectures*, vol. II, ch. X.
(39) URQUHART, p. 720.
(40) It is interesting to compare this conception with that of Prof. ALEXANDER, *Space, Time and Deity*, final chapter.

NOTES TO LECTURE III

(1) In "Church Historical Society Pamphlets."
(2) In *The Church and the Age*, ch. II.
(3) BEDE. *De Temporum ratione*, 15. See also at this point BRIGHT, *Early English Church History*, pp. 76–82 (text and notes), also Father DELEHAYE, *The Legends of the Saints*, and Bishop HEDLEY, *Treatise on the Holy Eucharist*, both in the Roman Catholic series known as "The Westminster Library," 1907.
(4) Bishop WHITEHEAD of Madras, now retired. *The Village Gods of South India*. Humphrey Milford, 1921.
(5) BRIGHT. *Op. cit.*
(6) DELEHAYE. *Op. cit.*
(7) VON HÜGEL, correspondence with Prof. Briggs over the Papal Commission and the Pentateuch.
(8) BRIGHT. *Op. cit.* p. 80.

162 NOTES

(9) JEVONS. *Introduction to the History of Religion.* Ch. XVI.
(10) DELEHAYE. *Op. cit.*
(11) LE ROY. *Dogme et Critique*, p. 26.
(12) PRATT. *Religions of India.* Chapter on Buddhism.
(13) INGE. *Outspoken Essays.* Series I, p. 221.
(14) A University sermon preached in 1924 by the Regius Professor of Divinity at Oxford, The Rev. H. L. GOUDGE, D.D.
(15) VON HÜGEL. Correspondence with Prof. Briggs.

NOTES TO LECTURE IV

(1) TROELTSCH. *Christian Thought, its history and application*, p. 26.
(2) TROELTSCH. *The Absolute Validity of Christianity.*
(3) HARNACK, in his *Ausbreitung des Christentums.*
(4) In a paper read at the annual conference of the Modern Churchmen's Union in 1923.
(5) A. LOISY. *Les mystères païens.* Final chapter.
(6) TROELTSCH. *Absolute Validity.*
(7) The figures are those of Prof. RAY LANKESTER.
(8) Cf. *The Ethical Teaching of Jesus*, by Dr E. F. SCOTT, of New York.
(9) In this connection cf. the article "Jesus" by Dr KIRSOPP LAKE in the *Hibbert Journal* for October, 1924.
(10) TROELTSCH. *Absolute Validity.*
(11) In a paper on "The Finality of Christianity," read before the Modern Churchmen's Union conference, 1923, by Prof. W. R. MATTHEWS, D.D., of King's College, London.
(12) See FOSDICK, *The Modern use of the Bible.* S.C.M. 1924.
(13) The following books are suggested in this connection as showing the tendencies of continental thought. All of them are small pamphlets:

> a. Adolf Harpf. *Amerika und die Religion der Zukunft. Kulturvergleichende Fernsichten.* 1913.
> b. Martin Schulze. *Die Forderung eines Zukunftsreligion und des Christentum.* Leipzig, 1913.
> c. Henri Constant. *Le Christ, le Christianisme et le religion de l'avenir.*

(14), (15) TROELTSCH. *Absolute Validity.*

For EU product safety concerns, contact us at Calle de José Abascal, 56–1°,
28003 Madrid, Spain or eugpsr@cambridge.org.

www.ingramcontent.com/pod-product-compliance
Ingram Content Group UK Ltd.
Pitfield, Milton Keynes, MK11 3LW, UK
UKHW020315140625
459647UK00018B/1882